Drawing & Painting Buildings

Reggie Stanton's Guide to

Drawing & Painting Buildings

Architectural Rendering

NORTH LIGHT PUBLISHERS
WESTPORT, CONNECTICUT 06880

Published by NORTH LIGHT PUBLISHERS, a division
of FLETCHER ART SERVICES, INC., 37 Franklin
Street, Westport, Conn. 06880.

Distributed to the trade by Van Nostrand Reinhold
Company, a division of Litton Educational Publishing,
Inc., 450 W. 33rd Street, New York, N.Y. 10001.

Manufactured in U.S.A.
First Printing 1978

Library of Congress Cataloging in Publication Data

Stanton, Reggie.
    Drawing & painting buildings.

    1. Architectural rendering — Technique.
I. Title. II. Title: Reggie Stanton's guide to
architectural rendering.
NA2780.S7   720'.28   78-11890
ISBN 0-89134-015-7

Edited by Walt Reed
Designed by Reggie Stanton
Composed in ten point Helvetica
by John W. Shields, Inc.
Color printing by Eastern Press
Printed and bound
by Halliday Lithograph Corporation

dedication

For the other team members.
Those two special ladies — my wife Doris
and our daughter Beverley. With love.

acknowledgements

Putting this book together has been a privilege and no small challenge. The task would have been totally insurmountable without help from the many fine people it is my good fortune to know.

Special thanks go to the late Abe Goldman, delineator and human being extraordinary, who first apprenticed me. To W.H.C. Simmonds for teaching how to read life's signposts. To Bill Fletcher and Walt Reed for their understanding, confidence and the right amount of encouragement. To Manfred Lopatka for pushing me in.

For their professional contributions, thanks are due to D.G. Williams —darkroom wizard, Rene Briggs and Bob Siegfried of Esquire Photographers, Austin Gilmore—best buyer in the business, Philip A. Crannell AIA., of Gee and Jenson, Stevens & Walton, Architects, Sheila Ross of Shiva Inc., Architect Gene Leedy, Journalist Jo (Dolly) Tanner and Calvie Hughson.

The talented architects and valued clients whose buildings appear throughout the book are gratefully acknowledged alongside the reproductions.

Extra special gratitude is due to my wife Doris and our daughter Beverley for their support and infinite number of sacrifices. From them came the source of spiritual sustenance.

Thank you U.S. of A. for taking us in.

Reggie Stanton
Winter Park, Florida

contents

introduction

An architectural rendering is a visual translation of an architect's concept. It is used as a selling tool to sell that concept at numerous stages before it can go forward. The rendering is part of a package that presents all pertinent information on the project to prospective investors — to government boards charged with controlling master planning, land use development, population density, landscaping requirements, parking etc., and to lending institutions for financial backing. After the building is completed, the rendering is still of immense value in the promotion of the project through brochures and advertisements.

The presentation package represents a considerable investment by the client in terms of time, effort, speculative land acquisition, feasibility analysis, surveys and architectural drawings. But through all this assembled data, attention zeros in on the rendering as the focal point of the entire pitch. The crucial visual communication in *layman terms* — the bottom line — ''What is it actually going to look like?'' To meet this requirement, our rendering has to be a literal, realistic and appealing picture of the building in its particular setting.

We have a unique art form here, an honest art calling for a unique combination of talents. The artist must also be a craftsman to understand and delineate precisely the various textures, materials and technical detail in order to make them 'read' convincingly. Also essential, is a feeling for the architectural statement being expressed together with a flair for landscape painting so that the building is displayed attractively in the desired mood and environment.

Ancient legend has it that the first drawing was done by tracing the shadow cast by an object on the ground. If so, that piece of artwork must have had a hint of one quality that eluded artists for thousands of years after — perspective. The principles of perspective, upon which is based the illusion of depth, distance, the effect of space on a two-dimensional surface, thwarted artists right through to the Renaissance.

1

The Greek philosopher Anaxagoras was referring to what we now call the picture plane when he wrote in the 5th century B.C., about "tracing on an imaginary intervening plane by a pencil of rays proceeding from the eye as fixed line of sight." If this was picked up by Greek architects to explain their classic concepts, no examples have survived. Greek art that has endured on their figured vases and friezes bears a resemblance to Egyptian wall paintings . . . everything in two-dimensional profile . . . elevations if you will. Vitruvius Pollio, an architect of the Roman Empire, referred to renderings in the 1st century B.C., but again no examples are known to have survived.

During the revival of architectural activity by the monasteries after the Dark Ages, design and building was in the hands of the monks themselves, a task that was later taken over by lay architects and master masons. The role of the mason increased in stature, and his skills were a major contribution to the construction of those incredible abbeys and cathedrals of the Gothic period. A considerable amount of creativity used to take place on the site itself, and although draftsmanship had developed to a high standard, knowledge of descriptive geometry and perspective was still non-existent. Situations not covered by the working drawings were explained with the aid of simple models. They had no need for renderings to sell their concepts (the local zoning and parking commission was probably off fighting in some Crusade anyway).

The Renaissance has been called the Age of Reason, when artists, sculptors and architects took a scientific approach in analyzing the underlying structure of everything they were depicting. Paolo Uccello (1397-1475), Andrea del Castagno (1397-1457) and Leonardo da Vinci (1452-1519) devoted a great deal of time researching perspective and geometry.

The architect had a need now for renderings. His main patron, the Church, wanted to see pictures of the building they were financing. A goldsmith, sculptor and architect, Filippo Brunelleschi (1379-1446) is credited with discovering perspective. It stemmed from his involvement in pictorially reconstructing ancient Roman ruins in an effort to unlock the secrets of their construction. Another artist-architect, Leon Alberti (1404-1472), was also concerned with recording the remains of ancient ruins, he too came up with a perspective system.

He used a model to demonstrate that if a three-dimensional area was divided into cubes by a grid, an object of known position could then be plotted in proper place on that grid in correct scale and proportion. He published his findings in 1435. His method of establishing the vanishing point was proved geometrically by Leonardo da Vinci, and came to be used by artists for centuries. The grid upon which the Adoration of the Magi **1** was constructed, could be one of the perspective grids of today that we will be dealing with later.

Expression of artist and architect were strongly linked throughout this period.

Donato Bramante (1444-1514), one of the first architects to design in perspective, was particularly concerned with giving a painted object the illusion of reality. He often allowed his talents to overlap by actually painting parts of his structures to achieve a desired illusion.

The rest of Europe became influenced by the Renaissance style, but more from an engineering standpoint rather than the artistic. Rendering was mostly in the form of tones applied to elevations and sections. Obviously there was still no call for a visual representation of how a building would look in perspective (some of those Crusades went into overtime).

Architectural rendering received a shot in the arm when pictures of existing buildings began to enjoy enormous public popularity, and artists were commissioned to make pictures of palaces, cathedrals, country mansions etc. An acknowledged master in this field was the Italian artist Giovanni Piranesi (1720-1778) who specialized in incredibly detailed renderings of buildings of the classic Roman period **2.**

When the graphite pencil as we know it was invented in 1795, architects appear to have found a medium they could really be comfortable with. The French in particular, and later the British, developed skills using the pencil, together with other media, and produced extremely effective renderings rich in intricate detail and realistic tonal values.

The development of rendering in the United States has a tradition that I find particularly stimulating. In the early part of this century, the education of an architect had more emphasis on art and drawing than is the case today. A course in architecture often involved a tour of Europe to study and sketch historic architecture. The drawing by Otto Eggars **3** was done on such a trip in 1912, and is reproduced here the same size of the original. These were the days before specialization, architects were their own delineators, and used their drawing skills to develop their design studies, Some of the renderings produced during this era are nothing short of masterful. I have always felt the pencil work of artist/architects like Otto Eggars, Schell Lewis **4**, Chester B. Price and A. Thornton Bishop deserves a wider public than just the architectural field. Reproductions can be found in old architectural books and old copies of the magazine *Pencil Points.* A present day student, in any branch of the graphic arts, could benefit immeasurably from exposure to the works of these artists. As someone who makes a living specializing in renderings, I find it a sobering lesson in humility to realize that architecture was their principal profession, and these brilliantly executed delineations merely a sideline. Many present day architects are also very talented artists.

It is interesting to observe how the changing architectural styles over the past few decades have influenced the mediums used to portray them. Pencil renderings, done well, have a unique, friendly, rustic quality. A client once told me that he would really prefer his houses rendered in pencil but was afraid they would appear old fashioned. The fact is, a lot of people prefer traditional type homes, and to my mind, the pencil still remains unsurpassed in depicting the charm of these styles of architecture. The bold lines of contemporary commercial buildings however — concrete masses and large expanses of glass — are a different story, they seem to come off best in opaque watercolor or line.

Opaque watercolor is a general term for a range of opaque paints having a water soluble base. It includes gouche, designers colors, poster paint and casein. They all have their individual characteristics, and all are used successfully by various delineators. I myself prefer casein. It thins to a nice 'buttery' consistency which suits my painting pace and gives me the crispness I need. I find I can handle areas of glass more effectively with transparent watercolor.

3

Pen and ink have been used in rendering for generations, of course. The old type of steel pen-point though, lacks a consistency of line and generally does not lend itself to modern presentation. The popularity of line renderings in recent years has been due to the development in Germany of the capillary type of mechanical pen. Known chiefly as the Rapidograph (but several other makes are available), they come in a range of line thicknesses, are consistent and fast.

You won't be very far into this book before realizing that my approach to renderings is a pretty literal one. This is no accident and I make no apologies. When the line 'artist's conception' appears below a reproduction of a rendering, there exists in the minds of some people, the ideas that this is another way of saying it is an exaggeration. There may have been justification in the past for this suspicion, promoters have been known to be prone to hyperbole. We have all seen announcements of a future building and wondered what feats of engineering genius were going to be called upon to fit it on to that site, because the rendering made it appear to be six blocks long. Not so today.

4

The age of consumerism — truth in advertising — is upon us, my friends. Your rendering can end up as Exhibit "A" in a court of law, because it shows a fifty-foot oak outside a condominium that someone has bought and is trying to un-buy. Most states today require that all photographs in sales brochures be taken actually on the site. Some leeway is allowed for renderings because obviously we're depicting something that does not yet exist, and small modifications often cannot be helped, hence the disclaimer. But we do have to faithfully represent the architectural facts and depict surroundings in character with actuality.

A rendering has to appeal to the people for whom it is made. The widespread use of photography, particularly color, has exerted great influence on peoples' perception. Under this spell. the layman can have trouble relating to a sophisticated, loose sketchy technique with acrylic streaks and bubbles. Once in a while I like to get involved in a project and follow it through to the zoning hearing. At one of these, a commissioner once expressed concern about some streaks of cloud shadow I'd used to break up a large area of stucco wall. He actually had to be assured they were not graphics that were going to be painted on the finished building.

A widely used modern sales tool is the color slide presentation. A lot of mileage can be obtained from a rendering with good detail by photographing parts of it in close-up. When these are projected in quick sequence, the viewer is very effectively taken in and out of the picture in almost a movie technique. One appreciates the value of detail when a figure that measures half an inch on the rendering is enlarged to a foot on the screen.

Students are always interested in the qualifications required to become an architectural delineator (that's a fancy word, but it sounds better than renderer). There is no set curriculum. I've yet to hear of a delineator who didn't back into the profession from another field. The delineator is more of a technical illustrator than a creative artist. He has an analytical eye for detail and is certainly different in outlook and temperament.

Anyway, what is creative art these days? A watercolorist with whom I was once chatting, suggested I should get into painting creatively to get away from doing the same thing day in and day out. We were standing by his exhibit — at least thirty pictures of barns. I suggested he get into rendering for the same reason.

Regarding qualifications, over the years I've found a brief run-down of influences in my own background explains it best. This is by no means a formula now, but I have been amazed by the parallels to other delineators with whom I've discussed this, so it may help.

I've always been intrigued with detail. Around tenth grade I made model ships and airplanes. Not content with just displaying them on stands, I strived for extra realism by painting backgrounds and photographed the models against them. Later I got into models in bottles. Not ships in big old whiskey bottles, but tiny every-day scenes inside aspirin bottles. Don't laugh, they helped put me through art school. Have fun while learning, as my daughter and I do, putting together models like the one used in the demonstration on pages 22-23.

The commercial art course I took after high school stressed hand lettering. We spent days duplicating typefaces with tiny brushes (very handy later on when writing away for sheets of transfer type). My gimmick was faithfully copying a cigarette pack at same size. That can discipline one's fingers.

Valuable experience in color matching was gained during a six-year apprenticeship in lithographic printing. I had to mix printing inks to match color swatches sent in by the salesmen. These could be anything from fragments of beer bottle labels to pieces of cork from a dartboard (a lot of printing business is conducted in pubs). Go through a magazine, cut holes in the middle of color pictures then mix dabs of colors to match exactly when placed behind the aperture.

I painted continuously in my spare time during these years. My passion was landscape and I sketched it during the back-pack trips I took throughout the British Isles, but mainly the industrial landscape of the English Midlands of which I was more a part.

Buildings fascinated me, and I'd walk through those cities on weekends from dawn till dusk, filling sketchbooks with buildings — good or ugly. Try it. Carry a sketchpad in your pocket and make use of those otherwise wasted minutes spent waiting around. There's no need to dwell on technique or style, just have fun, no one else need ever see the results. The most casual sketch however, will give you an insight into architectural elements that you'll find invaluable when rendering.

Well, for me, these influences finally came together. Do you see why you won't find a syllabus on the subject? You *have* found this book though, so I hope the following pages will prove to be a good substitute. I've presumed that anyone interested in the subject is already equipped with the fundamental basics of art, so I'll not be using up space with pictures of my water jug or tape dispenser. Areas such as composition or color theory are touched on as they come up, but really there are many fine books by authors far more qualified than I on those subjects.

Have fun with it. I do — in large measures — every single day. I'm surprised rendering is still legal.

perspective

Perspective, depicting three dimensional objects on a two dimensional surface, is the foundation of all realistic drawing. Don't allow yourself to be intimidated by the subject for one minute.

We were probably all introduced to the basics of perspective in grade school, remember drawing the scene opposite? This was demonstrating that all horizontal lines converge to a vanishing point on the horizon and that all dimensions appear to diminish with distance. We were guessing (eyeballing) the widths of windows and the distances between telephone poles. All we are doing now is using a perspective system merely as a tool that enables us to take the blueprints of that house and convert its dimensions to a fore-shortened condition. So that in the resulting three-dimensional view, all vertical lines are automatically spaced correctly as they recede.

The delineator has to be able to construct perspectives of a wide range of subjects. From small houses to skyscrapers to aerial views of large complexes. Don't be in awe of scale. The basic principles of perspective used to accurately depict the group of everyday objects at **1**, are the same ones upon which **2** is based. At **3**, they're just repeated a few dozen times.

There are many fine books on perspective theory, by all means read them, it's a fascinating subject. Many of them though, are highly technical and deal with many situations you'll never encounter. Using the methods in the following pages, the beginner will be surprised at how little practice is required before being able to handle any project.

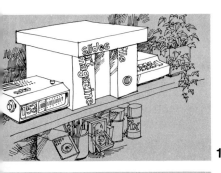

1

2

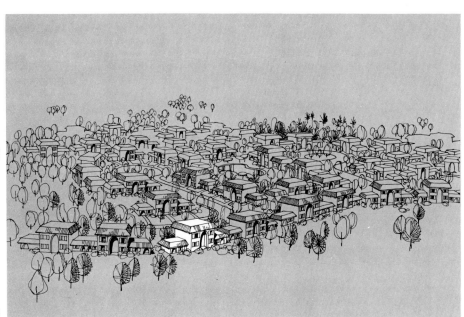

3

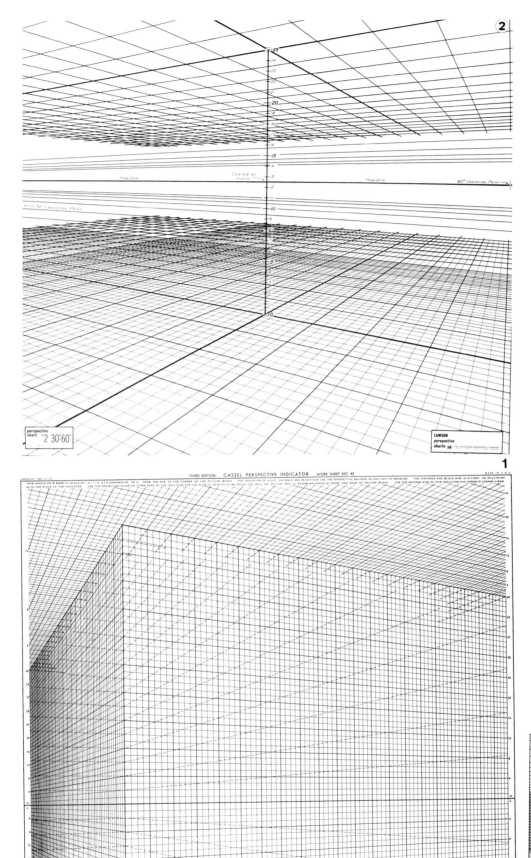

perspective
chart #2 30°:60°

LAWSON
perspective
charts VAN NOSTRAND REINHOLD COMPANY

1

2

charts

Each one of the methods we'll be dealing with can be used to construct every type of perspective. In practice though, you'll often find one kind of project lends itself to one particular method. You should, therefore, be familiar with all of them.

The charts shown here are very convenient tools. The perspective is constructed on tracing paper using the charts as underlay guides. The squares can be used as any unit of measure. All these charts are more flexible than they might appear at first glance, as demonstrated by the variety of projects at **3** and **4**.

The Lawson Charts **1**, are printed on eight separate sheets covering a range of angles and eye-levels. I find these charts favor aerial views where laying out in plan accounts for most of the construction.

The Cassel Perspective Indicators **2**, and GraphiCraft Multi-Grids **4**, are box type systems, using the front and side faces of a block as grids. The position of any parts of the subject, inside or outside of the block, can be plotted by projecting from the two faces.

The Cassel charts come in five sizes with four scales and are printed both sides of the sheet for opposite corner views. They can also be turned upside down for aerial views.

The GraphiCraft Multi-Grids consists of eight panels that can be interchanged in a variety of combinations to cover different situations.

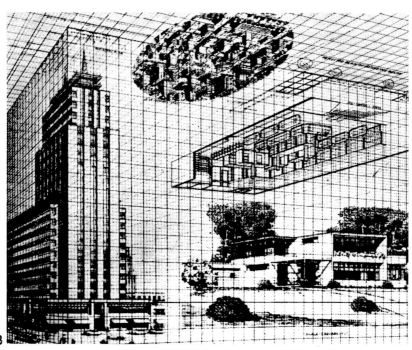

3

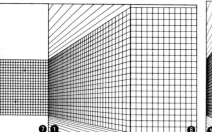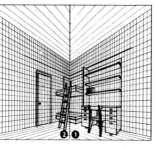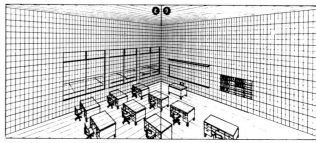

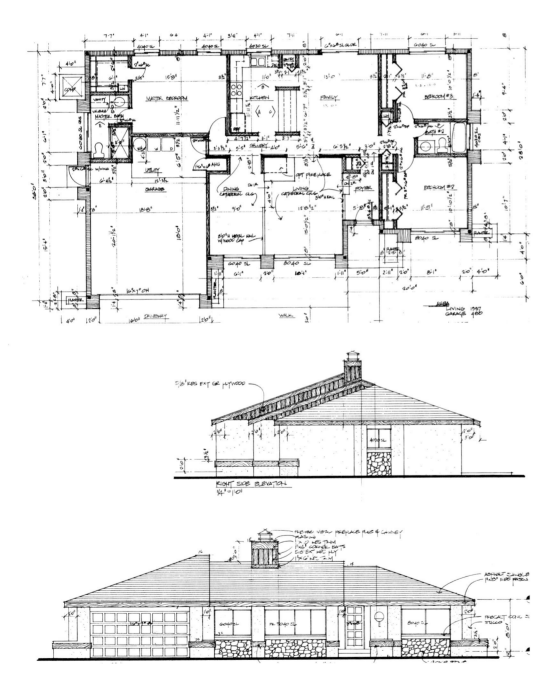

RIGHT SIDE ELEVATION
1/4" = 1'0"

The 20°-70° picture angle of the Cassel charts greatly favors the front of a building. This is ideal for most houses as it's not very often that there's much going on at the sides. The 20° angle would normally require one of the vanishing points to extend beyond the drawing board, but the grid feature eliminates this inconvenience.

The floor plan of this house shows that the front walls are arranged in a series of steps, so obviously it should be viewed from the side that looks *into* the angles. It makes measuring convenient to place one of these walls at the face of the picture block, leaving other parts to project into or out of the picture block.

The plan is drawn in *reflection* on the upper part of the chart, one square of the grid representing one foot. The front and side faces of the block are the measuring points from which elements *inside* the block are located e.g., the chimney, **A.** Parts of the plan *outside* the picture block are merely plotted directly on the grid of the horizontal plane, **B.**

The location of elements not indicated on the floor plan i.e., chimney and roof lines, are taken from the elevations. On some types of projects, we can find ourselves fighting a lot of criss-crossed lines. It helps to minimize confusion if some lines are drawn in different colors.

The perspective is completed by projecting lines down from the reflected plan. Horizontals are drawn where these intersect with the lines projected from the respective vertical dimensions, **C.** It's a help to indicate a little modeling as the perspective emerges, to define planes and materials.

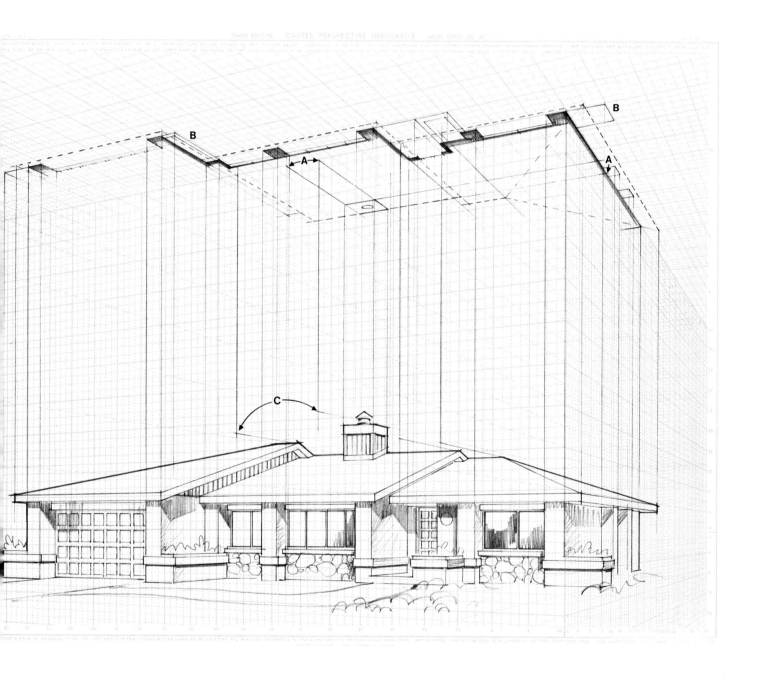

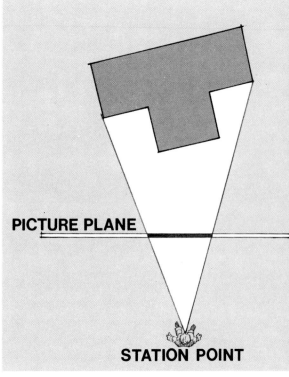

PICTURE PLANE

STATION POINT

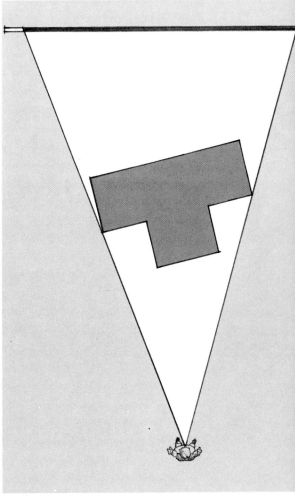

picture plane

The picture plane has nothing to do with 'in-flight' movies. If you look through a window at a building, then, with one eye closed, trace the image of it on the glass, you'll have a drawing in perspective of that building **1.** You've plotted where the rays between your eye and the building *pierce* the glass. Perspective comes from the Latin *perspicere* — "to see through."

If you draw a building in perspective on paper and hold it in front of you, you're seeing it just as if you were looking at it through a window. The picture plane then, is an imaginary plane on which the perspective is drawn. And all these years you'd been thinking that was just an ordinary old piece of paper you were drawing on.

In plan, this plane is shown as a line and is always at right angles to the direct line of vision. The diagrams **1** and **2** show how the size of the picture can be controlled by the location of the picture plane. The further away the picture plane is placed from the observer (station point), the larger the perspective will be.

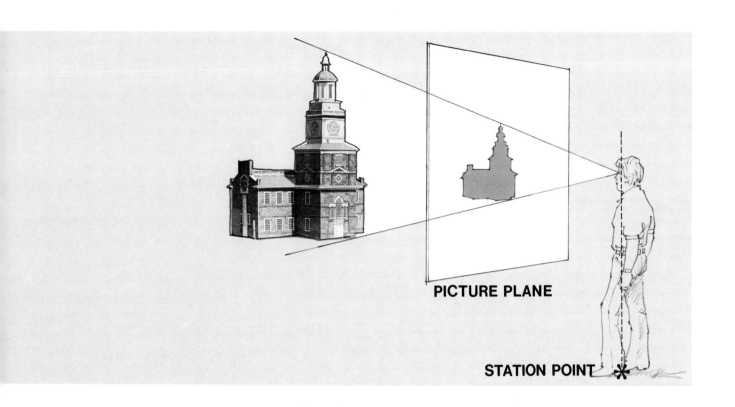

PICTURE PLANE

STATION POINT

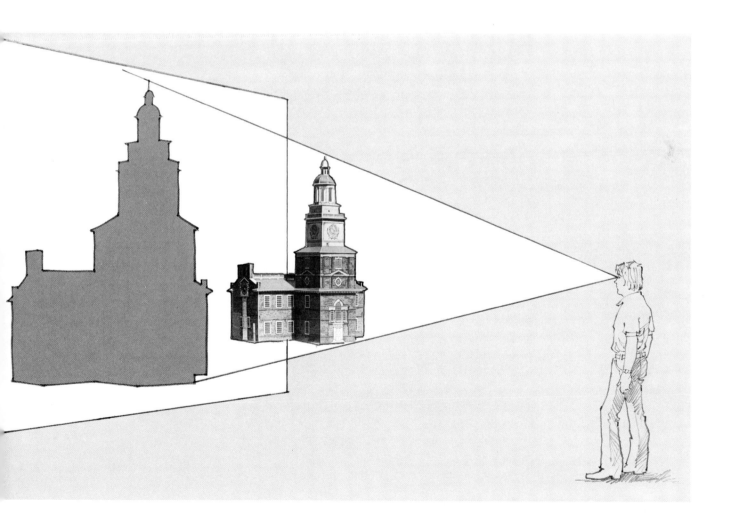

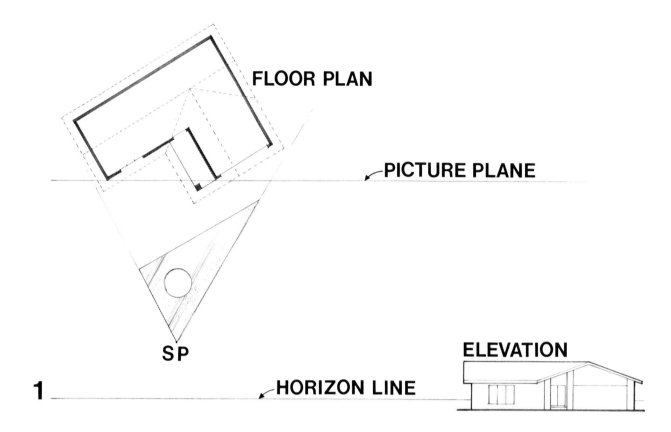

FLOOR PLAN

PICTURE PLANE

SP

ELEVATION

1 **HORIZON LINE**

the common method

This is perhaps the most widely used method of two-point perspective. Its simple basic set-up allows us to explore the effect of different viewpoints very quickly. The variables of station point, angle, and picture plane can be manipulated to show any building from any angle. We'll deal with this in succeeding pages, but first the basic set-up: —

1 . The floor plan is taped down at an angle under a sheet of tracing paper. The *station point* is determined by placing the 60° angle of a triangle below the center of the plan so that the width of the plan falls within the 60° cone of vision (page 27). Lines representing the *picture plane* and *horizon* are then drawn horizontally. For the sake of convenience, the picture plane is drawn here at the nearest corner of the plan.

2 . The two *vanishing points* are located on the horizon by drawing lines from the station point parallel to the sides of the plan. Then, at the points where they intersect the picture plane, vertical lines are dropped to the horizon-VPL and VPR.

3 . Lines are drawn connecting the station point with the various points on the plan, and vertical lines are dropped where these pierce the picture plane. Height dimensions are measured on the *height line*. This is a vertical line dropped from any point where picture plane and plan intersect, in this case at the near corner. Dimensions on this line are at the same scale as the plan and are projected back to their respective positions using the two vanishing points. The horizon is our eye-level, usually taken as five feet above ground line. If the building is to be depicted on level ground from a standing position, then height measurements should start at five feet below the horizon line. I think houses look better if slightly elevated; the horizon here is at three feet.

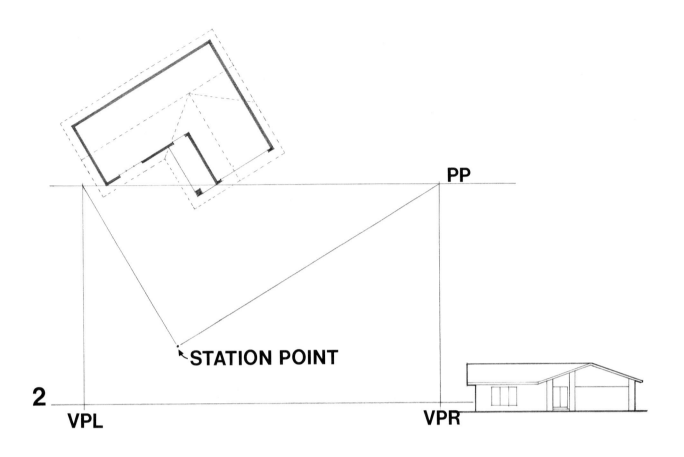

2

PP

STATION POINT

VPL   VPR

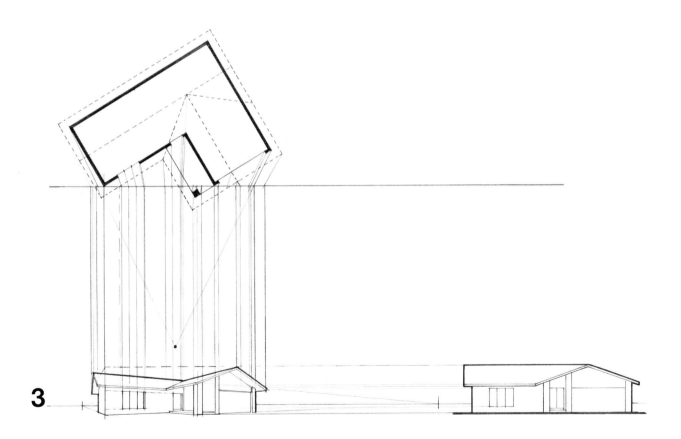

3

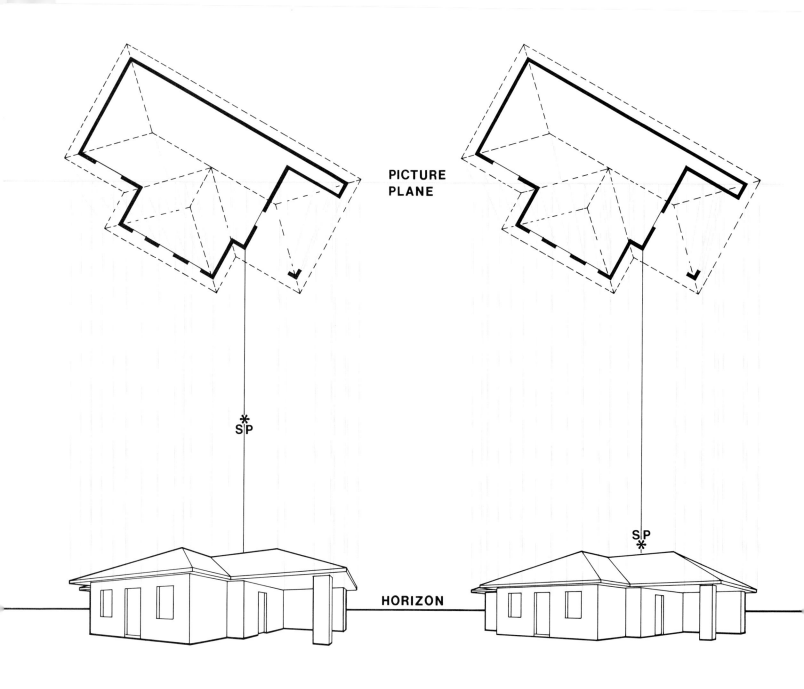

PICTURE PLANE

S|P

S|P

HORIZON

location of station point

The distance from the subject to the station point (how far from the building we're standing), obviously influences the pictorial effect.

Standing close to a building can give us good dramatic lines of perspective, but important parts of the structure can be hidden from view behind projecting elements because of this closeness. On the other hand, if we stand too far away, the angles of horizontal lines flatten out and become uninteresting.

We have to manipulate our station point so that we get maximum interest out of the building, while at the same time retaining as many of its features as possible.

In the view at left, we've lost nearly half of a house. The left end starts coming into view as we move back (center), but we have to move much further back before that element 'reads' to any extent (right).

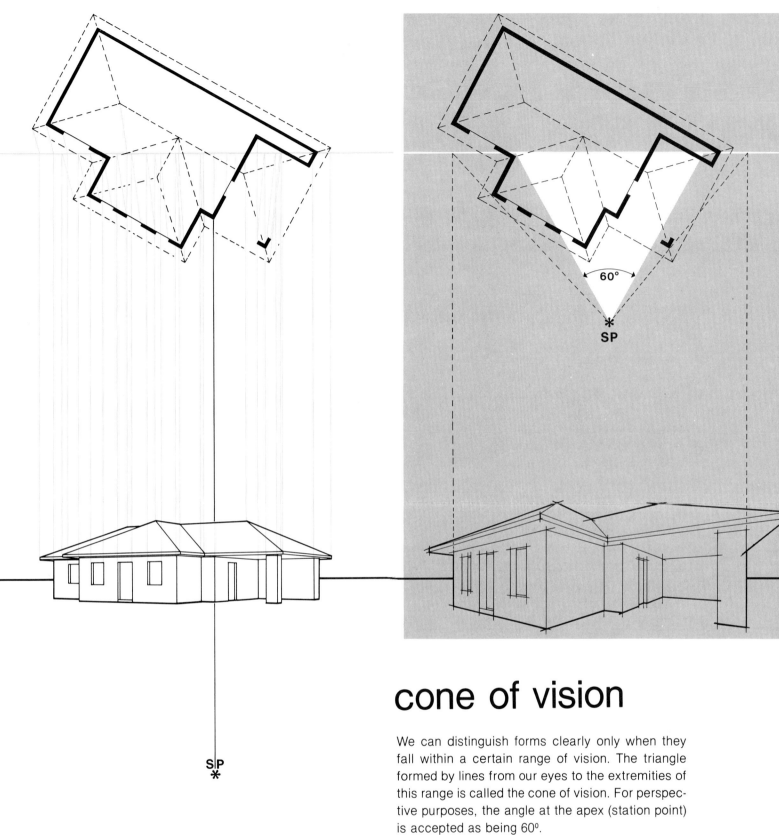

SP
*

60°

SP
*

cone of vision

We can distinguish forms clearly only when they fall within a certain range of vision. The triangle formed by lines from our eyes to the extremities of this range is called the cone of vision. For perspective purposes, the angle at the apex (station point) is accepted as being 60°.

In life, we constantly move our heads to bring other areas into our cone of vision in order to see them more clearly. A drawing however, can only look in *one* direction.

The obvious distortion, above, is the result of trying to depict areas outside the 60° cone. In other words, placing the station point too close to the subject.

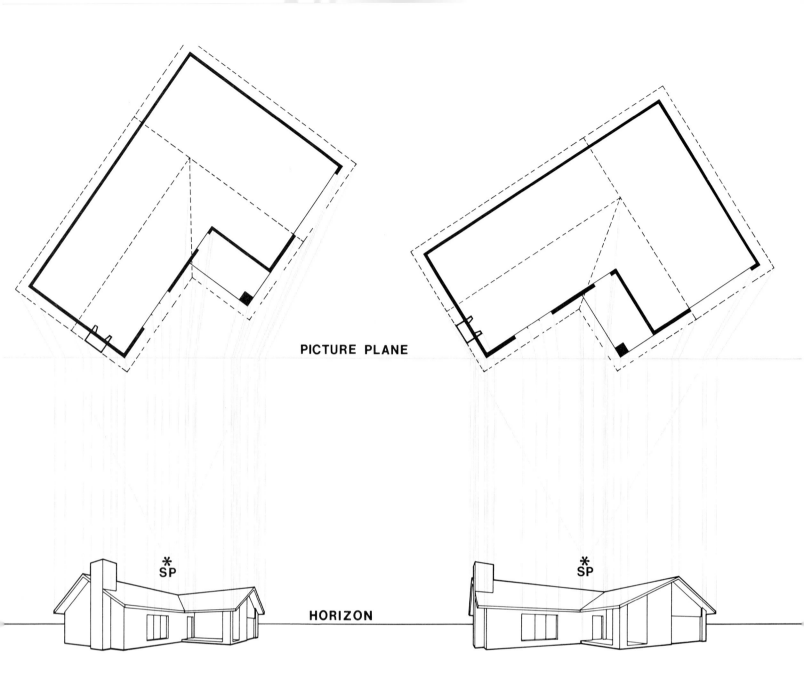

PICTURE PLANE

HORIZON

changing angle

The process of manipulating the variables of station point and angle is akin to taking a photograph of a building. If this were our task, we wouldn't think of shooting until we'd walked around and studied our subject from different angles.

A satisfactory viewpoint would be one from where we could see the maximum number of elements, particularly the entrance. Another consideration would be to keep structural lines 'open' and avoid corners clashing with one another.

Once familiar with the basic set-up of the common method, you'll find it takes only a few projected lines to get a whole series of quick outlines showing which elements are visible from various station points, (use a push-pin as a stop against which to pivot a straight edge). It's almost as if you're walking over the drawing board with a camera.

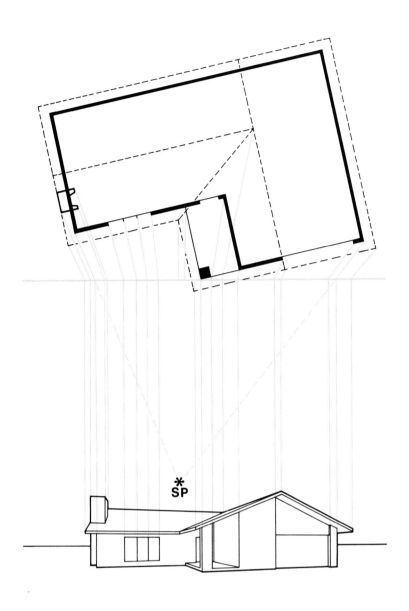

*
SP

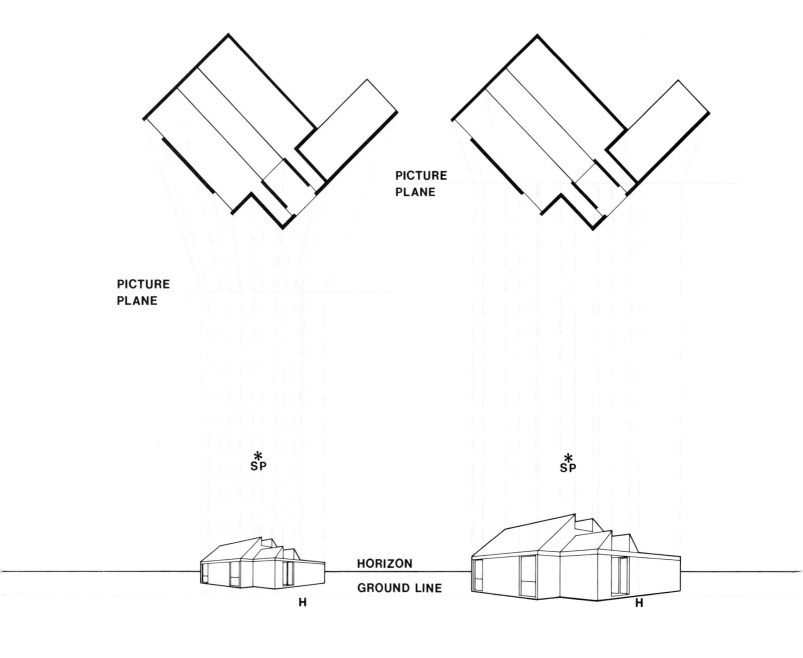

PICTURE PLANE

PICTURE PLANE

PICTURE PLANE

*SP

*SP

HORIZON

GROUND LINE

H

H

picture plane

Manipulation of angle and distance have given us control over our view of the subject, we can also regulate the *size* of that view with the position of the picture plane.

The closer the picture plane to the station point, the smaller the drawing will be (left). Moving the picture plane further away from the station point gives us a larger perspective (center and right), while retaining exactly the same view. Note how the height line **H** is determined when the picture plane doesn't intersect the plan (left and right).

This control over size gives the common method an edge over charts. Charts are constructed on a fixed plane, requiring any reduction or enlargement be done photographically.

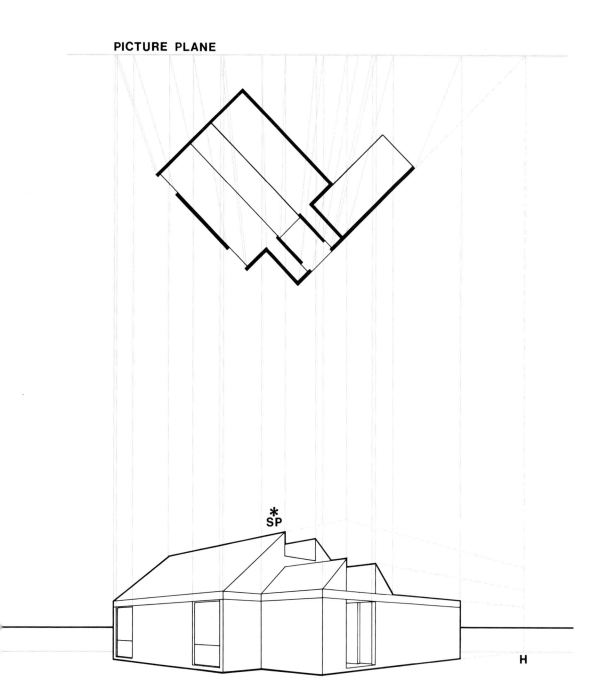

*
SP

H

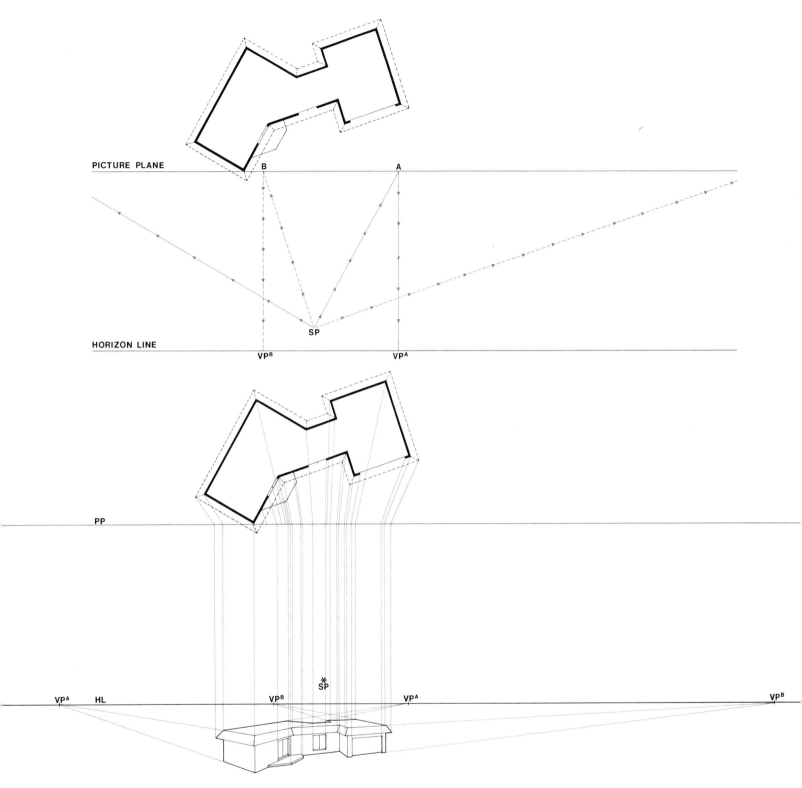

PICTURE PLANE

B   A

SP

HORIZON LINE

VP^B   VP^A

PP

VP^A HL   VP^B SP   VP^A   VP^B

angles

When structures have elements that are at angles other than 90º to each other in plan, extra sets of vanishing points are required. In the example here, set A is for the left side, set B for the right side.

Viewed from a normal eye-level, angles in a single story building show very little separation of perspective lines between elements. Looking down at the building (placing it below the horizon) gives a clearer 'reading' of this feature.

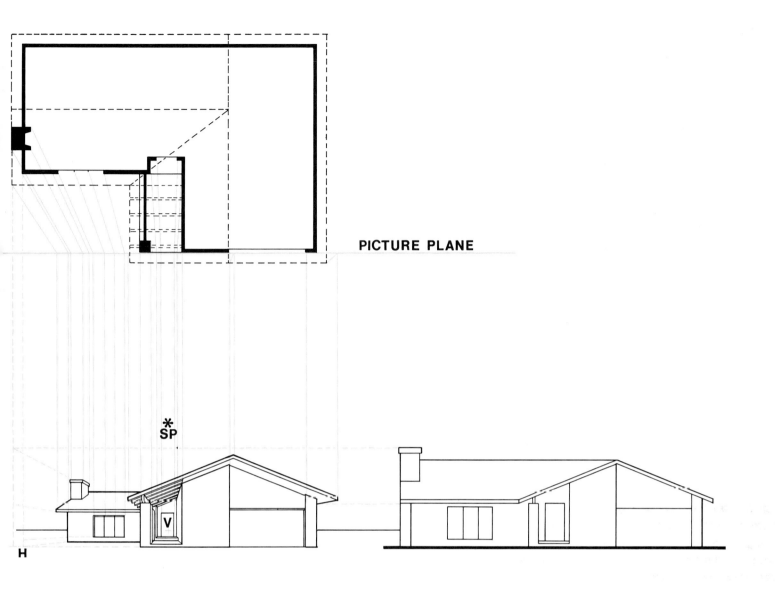

PICTURE PLANE

one point

In the methods we've used so far, the subjects have been viewed from an angle so we've needed two or more vanishing points. We've seen however, how frontal projections of buildings can block off other elements. The example above demonstrates how the one-point method can be used effectively to show an entrance that would be hidden if the house were depicted from an angle.

The basic set-up is the same as for the common method, the position of points being determined by where their projections to the station point intersect with the picture plane. All horizontal lines parallel to the picture plane remain horizontal. Horizontal lines vertical to the picture plane in plan, converge to the single vanishing point located on the horizon line perpendicular to the station point. Vertical dimensions are projected from a height line, **H**.

short cuts

There are times when it's necessary to make changes to an existing perspective and it's not possible to go back to the original work sheets. There may have been a change in size or the perspective was done elsewhere. There are a few tricks which can prove useful in such circumstances.

When an area is to be divided into equal spaces (right), draw a horizontal line from the corner. On this line, mark off the number of equal spaces required (in this case 5). These can be to any scale, ½"-1" etc. Draw a line from 5 through the corner of the face to the horizon. This establishes a special vanishing point which is then connected to the other numbers.

The points at which these lines intersect the top line of the face are the 5 equal spaces in perspective.

This same principle can also be used for unequal spacing (below). In this case the increments are units of any convenient scale.

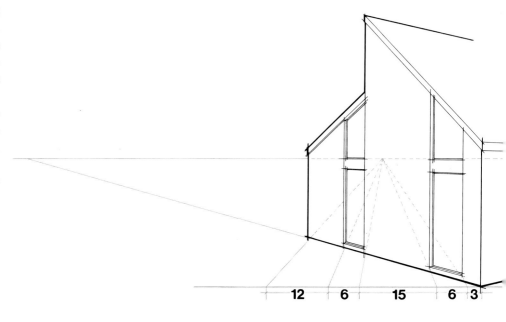

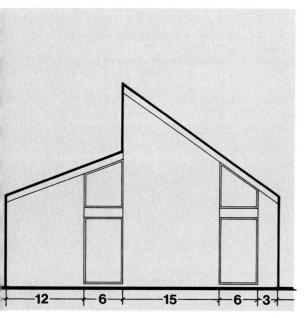

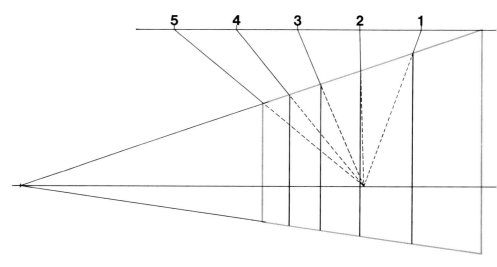

Another way of subdividing an area is by using a diagonal (right). Extend the top and bottom lines of the face to be divided. Then slide a ruler to a point where the width between these lines fits 5 convenient units on the ruler. Draw a vertical line at this point and mark off the 5 units, connect these to the vanishing point at left. Vertical lines through the intersection of these lines and the diagonal divide the face into 5 equal spaces in perspective.

Again, this method can be used for unequal spacing by using units of measure (below).

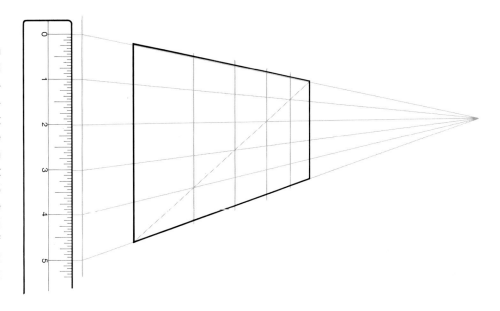

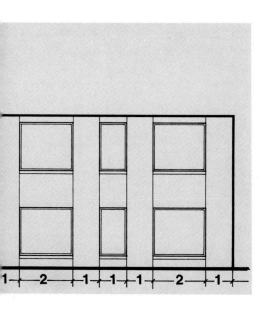

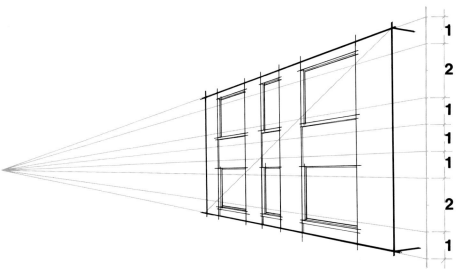

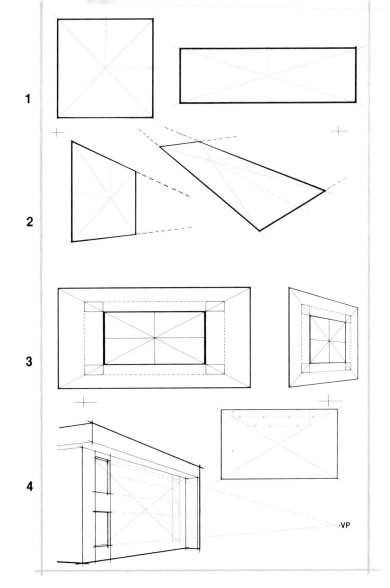

diagonals

The diagonal can be employed as the basis for a number of other useful short-cuts. The center of any square or rectangle for instance, can be determined by the intersection of their diagonals. Lines projected vertically or horizontally from the center will then locate the midpoint of the sides, **1.** This applies when the rectangle is in perspective, **2**.

At **3** we see how a symmetrical pattern can be projected 'around' a rectangle on its diagonals. A practical application of this would be in the situation at **4**, where a pair of windows has to be added to a wall at the same distance from the end as the existing pair. The new position is determined by projecting lines to the vanishing point from where lines of the existing windows intersect with the diagonals.

Repeating the diagonal method of halving an area gives divisions of quarters, eighths, etc., **5**.

5

The procedure at left dealt with using the diagonal to divide areas into equal spaces. But this can also be reversed and used to *add* equal spaces.

Lines are drawn to the vanishing point from the top and bottom of the area and also from the center of the verticals, **6a**. A line is then drawn from the bottom corner through the point where the center line crosses the other vertical and carried to the top line, **6b**. A line dropped from this point creates a second space equal to the first one. This procedure can be repeated to give any number of equal spaces in correct perspective.

In the example at **7**, the position of the two columns at the far end had been established. When the client decided to extend the trellis, the above method was used to establish the spacing of the added columns.

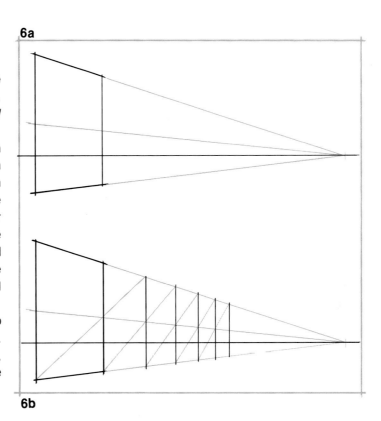

6a

6b

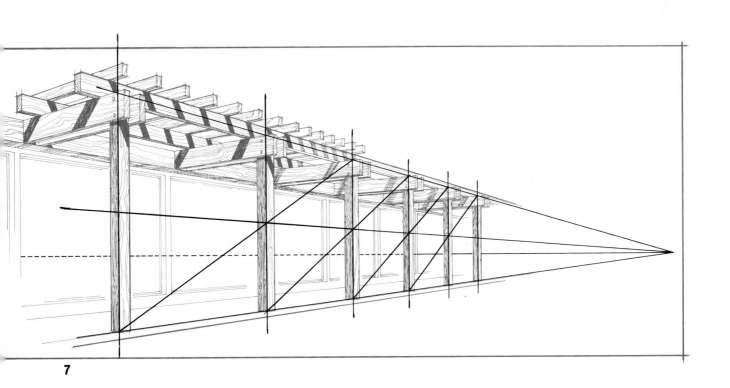

7

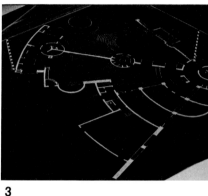

2

1

3

photographs

To construct accurate perspectives of buildings having the kinds of forms shown here, would have been extremely difficult, if not impossible, by any method other than photographically. For our purposes, it's not necessary to get involved with elaborate equipment or even a darkroom, we're only concerned with capturing an image on film upon which to base our drawing.

For the house at **1,** the floor plan was laid out on the drawing table, and two strips of card marked with the scale were placed at two points. Illumination was with two photoflood lamps. Using a 35mm single-lens reflex camera with a 1.4 lens, a series of exposures were then made from different viewpoints, **2.**

Processing of the film was carried out right in the office by loading the developing tank inside a cloth tank-loading bag (there's no need to climb into it, just your hands will suffice). The entire procedure took thirty minutes. A negative with the best viewpoint was selected, **3,** placed in a slide mount and projected up to the required size on a sheet of paper taped to the wall. Tracing the image produced the basic floor plan in perspective upon which the drawing was based.

models

Drawing the curves of the building at right, from a photo of its plan would still have required a considerable amount of 'eye-balling'. The problem was overcome by constructing this simple model. It was made in an hour using off-cuts of matt board, styrofoam and foam-core board, held together with white glue and pins. Construction was carried out on the site plan which had been pasted to a sheet of foam-core board. The walls and fascia were scored with a knife to facilitate the curvature. On the finished building, these surfaces were to be 4 ft. wide panels, so scoring at the joints served two purposes. Cars and figures were added for scale reference.

It's a good idea to photograph this kind of model outdoors in sunlight; this provides a valuable opportunity to study the effects of shadows cast by one form on to another.

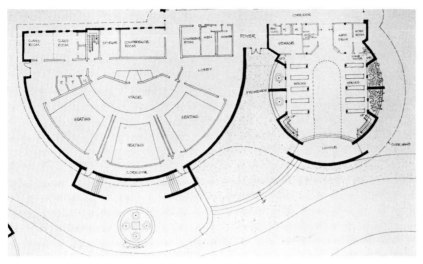

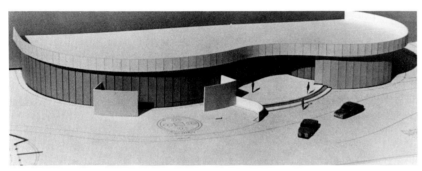

**Punta Gorda Isles, Inc., Punta Gorda, Florida

summing up

You now have a vocabulary of perspective methods that should enable you to tackle any type of project.

Don't let this aspect of rendering be a chore. There's a certain kind of beauty to perspective principles. Watching them work, as the project materializes right there on the drawing board, can be just as pleasureable as any other part of the rendering process.

A valuable side benefit of constructing your own perspectives is the insight gained from having to understand the building's various structural details. This allows you to plan how different situations can best be handled when you come to render them.

If the perspective is going to be submitted to the client for his approval, it's advisable to keep the work sheets and any alternative views that may have been explored. The perspective view of a building can be very different from the 'straight on' elevations and the architect is sometimes surprised when he sees how the perspective has brought out weaknesses in the design. Your work sheets will back you up should the accuracy of your perspective be brought into question.

MATERIALS

CUSTOM COLORS
3401-3410

3410 T - BLUE BIRD

3406 T - RIBBON BLUE

materials

Materials are *textures* the architect uses to control passages of color and contrast. They play just as important a role in the architectural statement as lines and forms.

A rendering should convey to the viewer a certain mood and atmosphere, and although this is created only by the artist feeling and experiencing this mood with every brush stroke, it is attained largely through the way in which surroundings are handled. The painting of the building itself really falls into the category of technical illustration. Remember those gorgeous illustrated brochures put out by the auto industry before they capitulated entirely to the camera? That's the kind of art we're talking about. The materials of a building are as specific and predetermined as the design itself, so their color and texture *must* be just as faithfully represented. The client is not impressed by an artist's interpretation of these areas any more than he would be if liberties were taken with the design.

Whenever possible, obtain actual samples of the materials and swatches of colors specified. When mixing your colors to match them though, bear in mind the principles of 'aerial perspective'. Colors seen from a distance lose their local color and appear lighter in tone and cooler in color as they recede. *Never* accept a verbal description of a color. A person's "kind of a pink sandy tan sort of on the beigey side" can be several spokes around the color-wheel from what he sees twenty painting hours later. Get him to commit himself with a swatch of some kind. The average executive is almost buried alive by magazines full of living color, put the scissors in his hand and get him snipping.

One of the great things about rendering is the fact that we are constantly surrounded by our own source material. Practically every material you'll ever be called upon to delineate exists on the buildings around you, just waiting to be studied every day. It's a good idea to familiarize yourself with as many examples as you can in your area. They can be valuable points of reference between you and your client when actual samples aren't available.

Make a habit of studying color photos in the architectural trade magazines. New materials are being introduced constantly, check the advertisements for them and write off for brochures, you'll find manufacturers invariably cooperative.

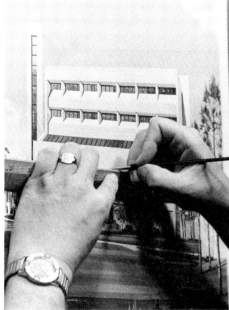

straight talk

"I can't even draw a straight line!" How often do you hear the expression? Well don't feel bad, the truth of the matter is, neither can anyone else. Not straight enough for our purposes anyway. We're going to be painting a lot of straight lines, so before we go any further, let's deal with them.

There's nothing better than a ruling pen of course for painting thin lines of uniform thickness, but this is not always convenient. The layer of paint on top of which the ruling needs to be done may be too soft for the pen to operate without clogging. Or you just plain can't be bothered to change over from brush—ruling pens can be cantankerous at times. There is an alternative method of painting straight lines that I'd like to demonstrate. If you're already familiar with it, please bear with me, a lot of folks are not.

The accompanying photographs demonstrate how straight lines can be drawn quickly with a brush, using the edge of a sturdy ruler as a guide. I've tried to photograph the procedure from enough angles that they'll be self explanatory. I'll just point out that the ruler is held in the left hand with the base in contact with the board. The three fingers underneath brace it firmly at an angle of about 45°. Hold the brush in the normal way, then position the fingers so that when the brush is lowered to where the line is to be drawn, the fingernail of the second finger and the metal ferrule of the brush form two points of contact with the ruler's edge. Sliding the brush smoothly along the edge while keeping angle and pressure consistent, produces a crisp straight line of uniform thickness.

This technique needn't be confined to just thin lines drawn with pointed brushes however. The variety of effects at left were achieved by varying pressure, jiggling the brush and swinging it back and forth as it moved along the ruler produced the curves. The examples in the lower half were painted with various square ended brushes and are strokes that I use when indicating shingles, bricks, glass, water and wood.

The illustration of the house, top left, was painted entirely with the ruler technique.

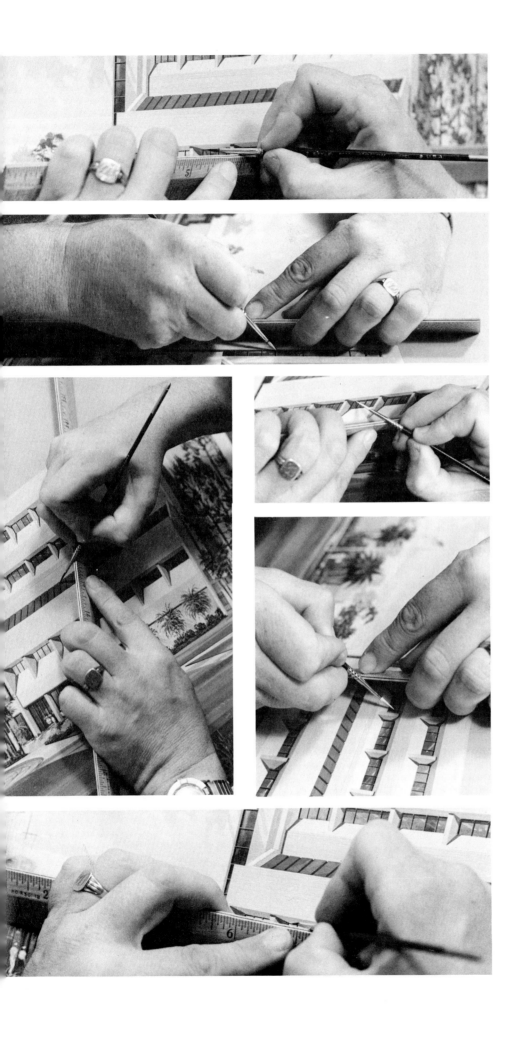

roofs

1

2

The easiest roofing material to render is undoubtedly composition shingle.

Fortunately for us it is also the most widely used.

In the painted demonstrations here, I'm using casein. This is an opaque medium, so I paint the background first then work forward. When working in line, I reverse this and draw the foreground elements first. I mention this procedure at this time because usually, roofs are in contact with the background more than any other part of the building. Consideration therefore, has to be given to the tonal relationship between the two prior to establishing the background. A light colored roof for instance, would be best displayed against dark foliage, while a darker roof would be better defined against a light sky.

The shape of individual barrel tiles, **1,** makes this a time-consuming type of roof to depict. The pattern created though, makes the effort worthwhile. When barrel tiles overlap it produces a stepped line. To indicate this step on every tile would take forever, so I reduce the rows to straight lines and suggest the courses with short dashes of different tones and a few curved edges. Accentuating the steps at the ridges and the hollow ends at the eaves, adequately conveys the overall texture and character.

Concrete tiles, **2,** have a good hefty feel. Emphasize their thickness at the ends also.

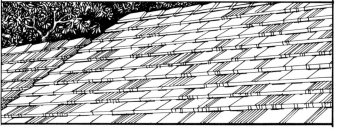

The basic color of this composition shingle roof is painted quite unevenly with a pretty thin mixture. I bring the nearer slope forward by painting it a lighter value than the one behind it. Streaks caused by rain wash are loosely worked in, these help to indicate the direction of the slopes.

Lines indicating the edges of the shingles are drawn with a ruling pen. Random breaks are made to avoid a mechanical look.

Some types of composition shingle have an interesting range of tones, while others are strictly a single overall tone. It helps to relieve the blandness of the latter with a few dashes of lighter and darker tones, put in with a squarer-ended brush. Some joints following the direction of the slope are then added with a small pointed brush.

1

I paint the overall tone thinly. A few streaks of a darker value are then added in the slope direction using a pretty dry brush dragged across the surface quickly.

2

shingle and shake

Shingles, **1.** are sawn from blocks of wood and have a relatively smooth mill finish. Their thickness is uniform and they are normally applied in straight courses.

Wood shakes **2.** have more character and are much thicker than shingles. They are split by hand from logs, this results in shakes which vary in thickness and a surface with a pronounced natural grain striation.

Shingles and shakes are sometimes stained, but more often than not are left natural. After a while, weathering takes place. This causes them to lose their natural color, take on a silvery appearance, and become curled at the edges, (don't we all). Shakes in any form have a beautifully rich, rustic quality that makes them a joy to render.

The edges of the shakes are drawn using the ruler technique. We have a foreshortened view of the shallower slope so the edges on this are painted closer together.

The irregularities of shakes causes light to fall on them at different angles. Some are relatively shaded while others reflect light to such a degree that they almost sparkle. Using a small square ended brush, I stroke on dashes of varying widths in the direction of the grain, first in the darker values then the lighter ones. I'm now thinking about that silvery quality, so I make some of the darker strokes a warmer tone and add blue to the lighter ones to reflect the sky color.

The all important texture and feeling of dimension is achieved when I add the dark lines representing joints and furrows of the grain with a pointed brush.

glass

New building materials are constantly being developed; none have been more dramatic than in the field of glass. Glass used to be just glass, but since we entered the age of energy efficiency, it comes tinted various colors like grey, bronze and gold. It can also be mirrored, **1** and **2.**

1

2

Mirrored glass is no problem to render, being just a reflection of the sky. Under some conditions, if it were not for the mullions, the building would be almost invisible. The planes are indicated by varying the tonal key as if the building is a great block of translucent material. When painting reflections in a mirrored glass a characteristic feature to consider is the distortion caused by surface aberrations, **3.** Other types of glass also reflect sky, particularly in the upper floors, **4,** so these areas are quite easy to depict.

3

4

What intimidates beginners about rendering glass is how complex it *appears* to be at lower levels, so let's analyze the factors involved — transparency and reflectivity. We're seeing objects *behind* the glass and reflections of objects *in front* of it. The complexity is due to the fact that we're seeing all these things superimposed on each other.

Let's approach the two separately and eliminate the extraneous in both. Reflection is adequately indicated by eliminating the reflections of everything except those objects in the immediate foreground. Likewise, it's not necessary to paint the entire contents of a room to convey transparency. This can be achieved with just a few highlights and features like other windows seen through the corners, **5.**

Above all — think glass!

5

I paint a general wash over all the glass area, starting light at the top and adding more pigment to darken it as I work to the bottom. Foliage reflections are then added in a darker value.

Now I start painting and thinking *through* the glass. I paint vertical streaks in a light tone to indicate drapes and stroke in a few highlights. Reflections of the mullions are painted with a ruling pen and their shadows painted on the drapes.

The windows are completed by adding the mullions using a ruling pen.

This is a commercial building with grey glass in a curtain-wall system. The glass on the shadow side reflects the sky and is painted much lighter than the front. Reflections of the fascia, mullions and the column at left are painted very dark.

Foliage reflections are painted on both sides. The ceiling light panels are painted with a square ended brush. These are part of the building's structure, so they're painted in correct perspective to add to the feeling of depth the other side of the glass.

The curtain wall material is set into the frame system on the same plane as the glass. This is painted next so that the mullions can be struck through both areas with the ruling pen.

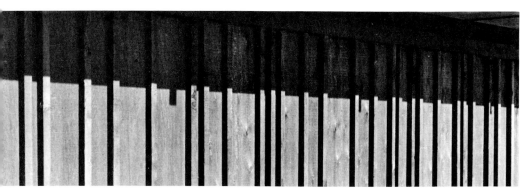

wood siding

The appearance of wood is subject to the effects of nature more than any other material we'll be delineating. This is usually taken into account by the architect when specifying wood type and treatments.

Left unfinished, some types of wood siding take on a patina and achieve a warm mellow quality. On other types, the rinsing action of rain causes them to become lighter in color and bleached to a driftwood gray. The architect sometimes prefers not to wait for this to occur naturally and specifies that the wood be treated with a bleaching agent.

Depicting the color of wood stains on our rendering requires a different approach than when matching solid paint swatches. Wood accepts stain pigments in varying degrees depending on which growth layer of the tree it comes from. This variation can be indicated by painting in a range of tones that express the general color when viewed as a whole.

The selection of wood treatment is usually relative to other materials or the surroundings, whether to be in contrast or harmony with them. There are clients who, even though the stain is intended to blend with a woodsey setting, still like the building to 'pop out' on the rendering. It's advisable to feel out clients on this point as changes can be difficult.

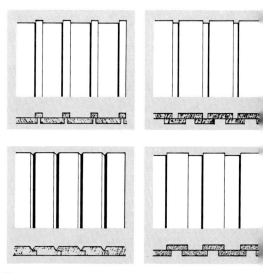

Four common types of wood siding:—
a. Board and batten.
b. Reverse board and batten.
c. Shiplap V-joint.
d. Board on board.

Working with a thin mixture and a square
ended brush, I apply the general color
in bands following grain direction.
I allow some overlapping of strokes
to achieve tonal variation while taking
care to avoid a candy-stripe look.
In the next step I add the grain
texture. This is done with a much darker
value by dragging an almost dry brush
across the surface.

Random dots are then put in with a
small pointed brush to indicate knots.
The battens are painted in opaque
color using a ruling pen. Projection
of the battens is emphasized by
stepping the edge of the shadow cast by
the overhang. Be sure to correctly
depict the style of siding specified,
1 X 8 boards with 1 X 2 battens, etc.

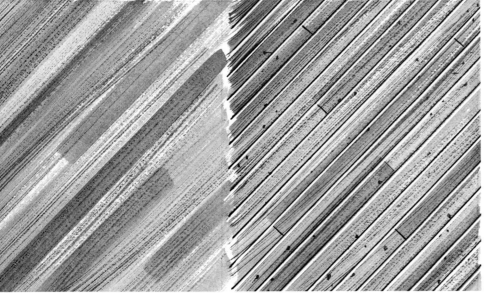

For this diagonal siding, the overall
range of colors and grain texture are
applied in the same way as above, but
two small differences are taken into
account. The variation in board lengths
result in random butt joints and this is
a smooth finish wood as opposed to
rough sawn, so grain texture is lighter.
The V-joints are painted with a ruling
pen in two tones, light on the face
of the V catching the light and dark
on the shaded face.

1

brick

There's no way out of this one. Brick is a time consumer. The other bad news is that brick is seldom mixed with other materials on a building as are stucco and wood for example. When the architect likes brick —Boy does he like brick—over the entire building. Be thankful it makes poor roofs.

There are a few types of brick whose coloration is accepted as pretty well standard and referred to as colonial red, Chicago number 3 etc. But when other types are specified, with so much work involved, it's almost essential to obtain actual samples.

1, 2, and **3** have a wide range of tones and colors from light buff to almost black, a feature that's not difficult to capture. A wall of bricks that are regular both in shape and coloring, **4** and **5,** can appear to be so even, when viewed from a distance, that it hardly reads as brick. This type calls for a lot of joint work.

2

3

These are some of the common bonding patterns one should be familiar with:

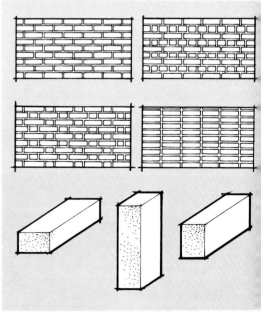

4

5

a. Running bond.   b. English bond.
c. Flemish bond.   d. Stack bond.
Add terms applied to various brick courses:
Header; soldier; rowlock.

The base color is painted quite unevenly. As in the other texture demonstrations, I apply this first stage with paint that's considerably diluted. This allows the 'tooth' of the board surface to be retained for subsequent stages.

I next put in the joints with a dark brown pencil. When painting the general color, I've allowed for the overall change in color and tone caused by this.

I add the range of lighter and darker values with a square ended brush. We're standing quite close to this wall, so the scale is such that I can add highlight lines along the top edges for added dimension. For walls at a smaller scale (below), I eliminate the finicky vertical joints and let the horizontal lines and dashes of different values carry the texture.

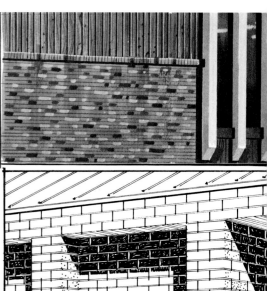

stone

Indicating surfaces has sometimes required that we exaggerate just a little bit to exploit texture and the illusion of dimension. Stonework possesses all the dimension and texture we could wish for. This is the one that, done well, elicits the—"wow, you can almost reach out and touch it" remarks from the layman.

There are many varieties of stone and as many different ways of laying them. In practice, and thanks to shipping costs, the delineator is usually called upon to render only the few that are native to a particular area.

The specimens at left are from Confederate country but are representative of the more commonly used types anywhere.

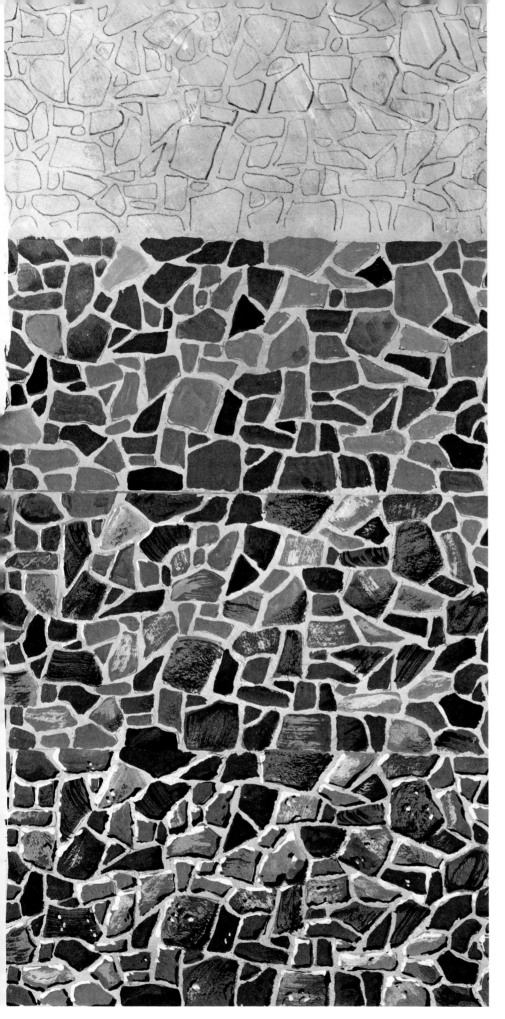

I paint a color representing the
mortar over the whole wall area.
In previous demonstrations, this first
stage has been painted with a thin
wash. This time I use a thick mixture
and apply the paint evenly with a
stipple action to build up a rough
texture. I then lightly sketch
the stone shapes.

I put in the stones with washes of
different values. I make a point, as
the mason does when he lays the stones,
to distribute lights and darks
in an interesting way.

Now the reason for painting the base
color thickly. Using an almost dry
brush stroked across the rough surface,
I model and texture the stones, in
varying degrees.

I finally add the shadows and
highlights to all the stones. I make
these more pronounced on some
to give them more dimension and
achieve variety.

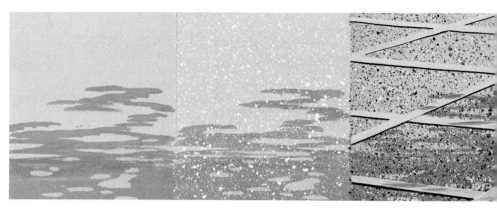

1

2

3

aggregate and stucco

At **1,** we have rough stucco. I paint the base color very thickly using a bristle brush, piling it on almost as if I were applying the actual stucco to a wall. I then load a brush with paint of a much lighter value and stroke it across the surface to create the highlights. This is adequate for some types of stucco, for types that are trowelled more heavily, I put in shadows under some highlights with a small pointed brush.

The material at **2** and **3** is aggregate—gravel, usually in a range of earth tones. For the pathway at 2, it's used as an infill between gridded form boards. At 3, as decorative panels on a fascia. To indicate the effect of all those pieces of gravel I call upon the old toothbrush splatter trick. Over the underpainting, I first splatter the light value followed by one or two darker values. Be sure to mask off the rest of the rendering before splattering, or you may end up with what appears to be flies swarming around your client's product.

The demonstrations have all involved three or more separate stages. Rather than concentrating on one material from start to finish, it's a good thing when possible, to paint the first stage of all of them. This helps to establish their values in proper relationship to each other and also provides a period of drying time before subsequent stages are added.

Any kind of material can be more convincingly depicted if something is known about its underlying structure. Learn about technicalities together with correct terminology from your builder clients, you'll find them helpful and respectful of your interest.

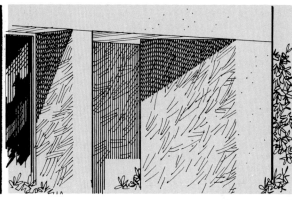

2   **3**   **4**

shadows

We've seen the value of shadows in giving dimension to surface textures. So much of the effect of architectural forms also depends on shadows.

Cast shadows are dependent on three factors—direction of light source, the shape of the form casting the shadow, and the nature of the surface on which the shadow falls. Using these principles, quite a lot of the story can be told with just shadows. In the analysis of shadows at **1,** we can tell that the window is boxed, has panelling above and a pot-shelf below, and that the wall is lap-siding headed with a beam.

Only objects in light can cast shadows and shadows can only fall on lighted surfaces. So if shadows are to be used to explain forms, the sun direction has to be thought out before rendering is started. At **2,** the shadows of the overhead members were needed in order for the structure to read as open trellis. Planning the direction of the sun so that it fell on the rear wall allowed this to be done, achieving, in effect, the luxury of a second viewpoint. At **3,** the shadows are placed so that they give emphasis to the projection of the pre-cast window elements.

4 is an example of shadows used to express form. The difference in the angles of the two elements is indicated by a corresponding difference in shadow angle. The shadow cast on the rear wall conveys the fact that a space exists between it and the element at right.

Shadow shapes are a combination of the form casting the shadow and the nature of the form on which it falls. Plotting them can sometimes be tricky. Whole books have been written on the subject—they'll make your head spin. A quick, easy way of resolving this type of problem is to reproduce the situation by taping together pieces of card, styrofoam, anything, then studying it in sunlight. (Any excuse to get into the big outdoors).

TREES
FOREGROUND LIMBS

entourage

Entourage is the French word that encompasses surroundings, environment, atmosphere, setting etc., for which no inclusive word exists in English. Sky, landscaping, people and cars all play a role in telling our story — supporting roles. Our principle players are trees. They *must* be handled well! In more cases than architects would probably care to admit, good trees have 'made' a rendering.

When all that technical stuff becomes uninspiring, when the artist in us protests the disciplined routineness, trees provide the compensation — the cool one at the nineteenth. Joyce Kilmer was right of course, but don't let what he said about trees stop you from at least trying to make them. It didn't stop Disney World.

Architecture and materials are depicted better when they're understood. Understanding is also a requisite of portraying trees well, but with such gorgeous subject matter, an infinitely more pleasurable process. Any subject can be so much more successfully depicted when the artist feels sincere affection for it. And who can feel anything but affection for trees? One of man's most loyal living friends — our greatest natural resource (the only renewable one) — providers of innumerable benefits to us through the centuries. Any setting benefits from their presence, not the least being architecture.

My infatuation with trees was kindled in the fifth grade by a tree lover named Mr. Wareham, a Dickensian character complete with pince-nez and wing collar. Mr. Wareham was the supervisor of art instruction for our school system in the industrial Midlands of England (tree population three per square mile). On his visits with us he'd gather us round him on the hearth in front of the open fire and treat us to the most wonderfully entertaining chalk talks on trees and things. I think of him every day as I use those basic V's of tree structure and thank goodness our school was one of the few with a fire. I'm sure it was the reason for the frequency and duration of his visits.

I'll be demonstrating my own approach to the portraying of trees but really, there is no substitute for direct observation of nature. Go out and just draw the darlings — lots of them — many times.

Mid morning and late afternoon are good hours for studying trees. The low sun angle gives emphasis to the foliage masses and illuminates the trunks and limbs nicely. Strike up an acquaintance with your friendly neighborhood oak and observe it under different conditions throughout the seasons.

From a practical standpoint, it's not necessary to be totally familiar with all that many types (considering there are 865 species in the United States). A vocabulary of trees for general rendering purposes need only be comprised of types that cover a range of diverse silhouettes and branch structures such as the ones dealt with in this chapter.

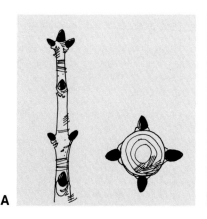

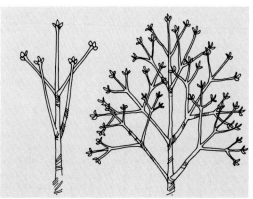

A

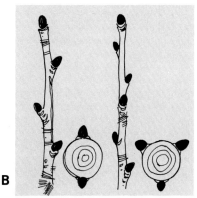

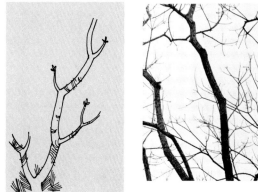

B

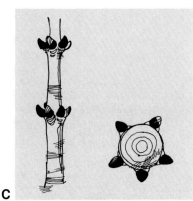

C

tree structure

The trees in a rendering should look natural, but like Whistler said—nature is never right. Some parts have to be moved, some simplified and others eliminated. (He falls in love with them and straight away he wants to change them).

Each species has its own personality and in manipulating it to our requirements the characteristics of the particular tree "type" have to be retained. This flexibility can only be achieved by understanding the natural laws governing their structure. Just as drawing the human figure in action requires some knowledge of anatomy.

The definitive work on the subject is "The Artistic Anatomy of Trees" by Rex Vicat Cole, first published in 1915. It is to this work that acknowledgements are due for the following.

The structural patterns that different species conform to are consistent throughout their growth right down to the way the buds are arranged on the twigs. There are several types of arrangements, the three most common being: —

A. **Opposite buds.** The buds grow in pairs on opposite sides of the twig with each pair at right angles to the pair above and below it. Sycamore and Maple follow this arrangement. If all shoots came to maturity it would result in crowding. But what happens in actuality is that one or two shoots die for want of light and air, leaving the survivors to grow either equally or with one becoming the leader. It is the shoots that don't make it that account for those insignificant twigs and characteristic projections at the elbows.

B . **Buds arranged singly.** This arrangement results in limbs that zig-zag like those of the Elm. On some species, the buds alternate on opposite sides. On others, like the Oaks, they spring from 3 or 5 sides.

C . **Buds crowded in groups.** The Pines and Spruce follow this arrangement. The shoots are clustered around the main trunk at intervals.

It follows that these arrangements produce consistencies of branch formation peculiar to a particular species throughout its growth, a limb being just a twig that has grown old. The examples here bear this out.

Just look at the similarity between the twigs and the older trees they were taken from, in both the structure of the branches and the angles between them. The twig photos could almost have been taken of the older trees at the time they were planted—fascinating. Make a few detailed studies of twig clusters. They don't have the "character" of mature limbs of course, but they will teach you much that you need to know about such things as the rate of diminishing thickness, angles of separation and the comparative thicknesses.

Another natural law that affects the form taken by limbs is the process known as *phototropism.* All plants produce growth hormones called auxins. The action of light destroys the auxins on the sides of the twigs exposed to it. The auxins on the shaded side, reinforced by some that have migrated from the other side, then induce a higher growth rate than the lighted side. This causes the stem to bend in the direction of the light resulting in those graceful curves that are characteristic of a tree's lower branches, **1** and **2.**

1

The influence of phototropism is also apparent in the overall tree structure. The growth toward light process causes the topmost branches to point upwards, the middle ones outwards and the lower ones downwards. Thickly massed trees tend to have taller and straighter trunks with all branches reaching up towards the light. When two or three trees grow close together, they tend to lean away from each others' shadows and most of their growth seeks light on the outside of the group.

Sorry about the biological mini-treatise. But I hope you already feel prepared to portray our friends with more authority.

2

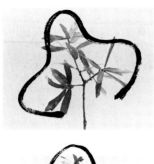

1   2   3

foliage

Trees are not the riotous vegetable explosions they may appear to resemble. There *is* some order there. If there weren't, I'd be able to slap them in with a sponge and go home early enough to catch the late night movie occasionally. Boy, how I've tried.

Having hopefully opened your eyes to tree structure, I suggest that when looking at foliage you do so with them half closed. This will help to filter out the intimidating deluge of detail and see the order of foliage "groups".

Instructions on depicting trees in a landscape application usually prescribes simplifying foliage masses to their broadest aspects. This is fine for trees that are part of a landscape that's also treated broadly. In a "tight" rendering however, where we're committed to precise architectural detail, the surroundings must also be depicted with some degree of detail if the picture is to have a homogeneous quality. The masses of distant trees can be handled broadly, but the trees that play a more predominant role have to be developed a stage further. We're not talking about delineating every leaf, just giving "leafy character" to the foliage groups.

The artist's approach to nature's more complex forms has always been to establish some consistencies of rhythm or pattern, some rules-of-thumb. The use of such patterns in depicting foliage not only helps in attaining some semblance of order, but also achieves the desired quality of cohesiveness.

A pattern that I use is based on a maple leaf-like shape that is apparent in the smallest leaf clusters, **1,** then right through to the outlines of larger foliage masses, **2.** I've noticed this shape prevails in a surprising number of species, including even palms, **3.** This shape happens to work for me, your squint-eyed observations will probably reveal others. You never know what you'll stumblé into wandering around the countryside with your eyes half closed.

Study the shapes formed by the "sprays" of leaves, opposite top. Observe the interplay between their lighter shapes and the darker ones of the interior as they criss-cross around the tree. Look at that light colored new growth at the tips — it twinkles.

The methods I use to depict foliage texture with paint will be covered in the demonstrations following. Pen and ink calls for a different approach of course. The secret here is to work with a pattern that gives appropriate texture, tonal gradation and allows large areas to be covered quickly. As shown at right, there are any number of ways to go.

1

oaks

To study individual trees at their best you really have to search out isolated specimens whose growth is unimpeded by competition from others. They can be found in places like meadows, public parks, or my favorite hunting ground —golf courses, where they're treated to a steady diet of nutrients.

When we put trees into renderings we're idealizing to a large extent. The limbs of oaks for instance, are painted throughout with all the characteristic twists and 75°-90° angles, and with large openings in all the right places. In nature however, such perfection rarely exists. Limbs aren't always conveniently displayed against openings and sideways views of forks narrow their angles so that they resemble those of an elm more than those of oaks, **1.** The foliage on others may be so dense that no openings or limbs are visible at all, **2.** So we use a little license and rearrange nature a little.

I start by painting the tree in dark silhouette. Establishing the pattern of foliage masses first, then the skeleton structure.

3

The big secret of tree painting—and this applies to limbs and foliage—is to manipulate the brushes so that they do the work for you. Don't try to paint individual leaves. It would take forever and still not look natural. I paint the foliage here with semi-dry paint that allows the brush to produce the broken edge that suggests thousands of leaves with one stroke.

When painting the branches, I find that I can express their character easier, particularly at the elbows, by *pushing* the brush in the direction of the growth, **3.** Any overlapping of branches is kept 'open' so that the negative shapes form a pleasing pattern.

Using a middle value, I then paint the lighter masses of foliage and the branches that fall in front of the darker ones. I've now established some degree of dimension with shapes in two values. The final stage is one of modeling those shapes with lighter and darker values.

I put in light values on the trunk and branches, at the same time adding a few extra sideshoots here and there. I then model with darker values and add the shadows cast by foliage and other limbs. Finally I model the foliage with lighter values. Again I allow the larger brush to do the work of expressing leaf texture, but use a small brush to sparkle up edges here and there.

2

1 2 3 4

pines

The distinctive features of the pine family are the single vertical trunk and horizontal branches. As a composition tool, the vertical trunk doesn't afford us the flexibility that we enjoy with trees. Care has to be taken in their placement to avoid clashing with vertical elements of buildings.

I find the spruces and firs with their church-spire crowns, the most visually pleasing species but they're confined to the far northern and western regions.

The more common species of other areas are enough alike for our purposes to be typified by the Shortleaf Pine, **1** and **2,** and the Slash Pine, **3** and **4.** You'll occasionally come across a dead evergreen, **5,** take the opportunity to study its structure.

A characteristic feature to remember when painting the trunk are those broken off side-shoots. These are the result of the pine being incapable of replacing limbs lost over the years like most other trees can.

When modeling the silhouette, bear in mind that the foliage masses are distributed around the trunk. Leave the ones on the far side in a dark value, then display the trunk and branches against them with lighter values.

When drawing pines in pen and ink, I like to exploit the predictability of the vertical trunk by losing the outline here and there. This heightens the effect of sunlight.

5

1

landscape trees

It may have come to your attention that all building sites are not exactly blessed with a built-in sylvan thicket of majestic oaks. The delineator very often has to work with a site which could have qualified for Neil Armstrong's moon-walking practice.

Developers have become sensitive to 'truth in advertising' pressures. Renderings are now required to reasonably represent the product offered. In the absence of existing trees on a specific site, this restricts us to specimens that could be planted as part of the overall landscaping. We're deprived of those trees in back of a building that normally account for the majority of trees in a rendering and that are so useful composition-wise.

We have some degree of latitude in the depiction of young trees. It's not expected that we show them as they appear on the day they are planted, two or three seasons' maturity is acceptable. The fact that trees in this situation are confined to the front of a building does make their placement more critical, blocking off important areas of the building with foliage mass has to be avoided. One way is to make use of young saplings with lacy foliage, **1** and **2.**

A common problem with young trees is their lack of character. A little manipulation is required to make them interesting. The tree at **3** has the makings of a pleasing branch formation but its foliage mass is just a blob. The foliage of **4** has attractive form and outline but the trunk is just a post. The drawings on the opposite page result from combining the better qualities of both. The tree on the left is against a light background so I used a thick pen and achieved the contrasting dark value by keeping the lines close together. The one to the right was drawn with a more open texture using a thinner pen so that the light value would contrast with the darkness of the background.

2

3

4

1   **2**   **3**   **4**

palms

These are the romantic mood setters. I realize they're regional, but their omission here would put me in bad with the local Chamber of Commerce. For clients in appropriate areas, their inclusion in a rendering is practically mandatory. It's a symbolic value. One palm frond in a rendering and the message flashed across the screen says 'halcyon tranquility and sunshine'—pretty attractive selling points.

There are two types of fronds. One type is shaped like a fan—Washington Palm **1,** and the more common Cabbage Palm **2,** are examples. The other type has a feather-like formation and is represented here on the Date Palm **3,** Coconut Palm **4,** Royal Palm **5** and Queen Palm **6.**

Landscape architects usually arrange Cabbage Palms in groups of three or five with an interesting variation of heights. Their leaves present quite a complex mass to depict in line. My approach is to build up the texture with short radiating lines then model with cross-hatching, much the same way as I draw pine needles.

I paint both types of leaves with a round brush whose bristles I've fanned out by pressing them on to the palette as I pick up the paint. Palm leaves have a smooth shiny surface, so I highlight some with a bluish cast and add a few accents of white to indicate reflected sunlight. The symmetry of some palms to me, gives them a stately bearing, but I think Coconut Palms are more attractive when their symmetry is offset by having the trunk lean at an angle and the fronds swaying to one side. It has something to do with the relationship between the large mass of fronds and the slenderness of the trunk. In the line drawings of fronds, which in a rendering would be a foreground overhang, I've allowed the background leaves that are in shadow to determine the outlines of some of the nearer ones. This emphasizes tonal contrast consistent with tropical sunlight.

The trunks of palms are normally a light driftwood grey in color, highlighted virtually to white in sunlight, and characterized by horizontal rings. They lack the 'woodiness' of other trees and have a tubular, almost metallic look.

70

5

6

groupies

Trees forming the backdrop to small buildings like single-family residences are most often painted in groups rather than isolated specimens. They are put in before the house is, so it has to be decided if a dark background is needed to display a light roof or vice versa.

In groupings, right center, the foliage masses are so intertwined that their placement requires little consideration. The silhouette here is blocked in with a dark value, painting quickly and loosely in extemporaneous fashion. Limbs are then painted to the foliage masses, capitalizing on accidental effects that may have occurred. The trees are finally modeled with lighter values, again quite freely. I find groups handled in this way have an informal natural quality.

When trees are planned for the front of the house, background masses should be kept simple and preferably in a middle value that allows for both light and dark values to be shown against it, bottom left.

The groupings at right, bottom, demonstrate another treatment I sometimes use. Here the foliage is painted throughout with a small square-ended brush. Foliage texture is achieved by applying the paint in a pattern of dabs working from dark to light. The light openings in the distant tree mass are put in with the same brush. Painting them with the brush well loaded produces the rounded shapes that give a diffused out-of-focus effect and enhances distance.

73

1   **2**   **3**   **4**

trunks

Any rendered subject invariably benefits from being 'framed' by one or two trees in the immediate foreground. They create a feeling of scale and an illusion of depth. Also, as a composition device, their vertical lines serve to counteract the influence of horizontal lines that can lead the eye out of the picture.

The trunks of trees in the middle distance have been modeled in just broad planes. When portraying trunks at a larger scale however, we have to consider texture. So we should be familiar with a range of bark characteristics and treatments.

Trees in the Northern Hemisphere twist in a clockwise direction as they grow. So any vertical flutings indicated should slant from left to right upwards from the bole, **1.** When vertical trunks are illuminated by a high sun-angle, their roundness has an uninteresting regularity. Painted this way, they lack 'woodiness' and have almost a man-made appearance. Study them when the sun angle is low and note how the planes are so much better defined, as in the photo of the pine at **2.**

Pine trunks are characterized by rectangular shaped scales set vertically in almost a brick formation and separated with dark rivulets, right.

The line drawing at far right is a decorative treatment of bark scales I use from time to time for the type indicated in photos **3** and **4.** Roundness is suggested by foreshortening the shapes as they pass around the sides.

The palm trunk illustrates how the creation of divergent angles can bring some degree of drama to an otherwise plain old ordinary structure. It doesn't necessarily have to be a palm of course, any trunk can be used this way, or any element that's relevant if it comes to that. I've used the boom of a sailing boat several times. When modeling the palm, a strip of reflected light along the side in shadow conveys the smooth round form. The lateral rings are put in with a square-ended brush and a few random bird-pecked holes added.

In the line drawing far right, note how the rings are ellipsed to indicate the sweeping curves towards and away from you.

At right are three other texture types in line. The one on the left shows a quick method of achieving a dark value while at the same time suggesting bark texture. A series of wavy lines are drawn with a thick pen, then cross-hatched with another set of wavy lines.

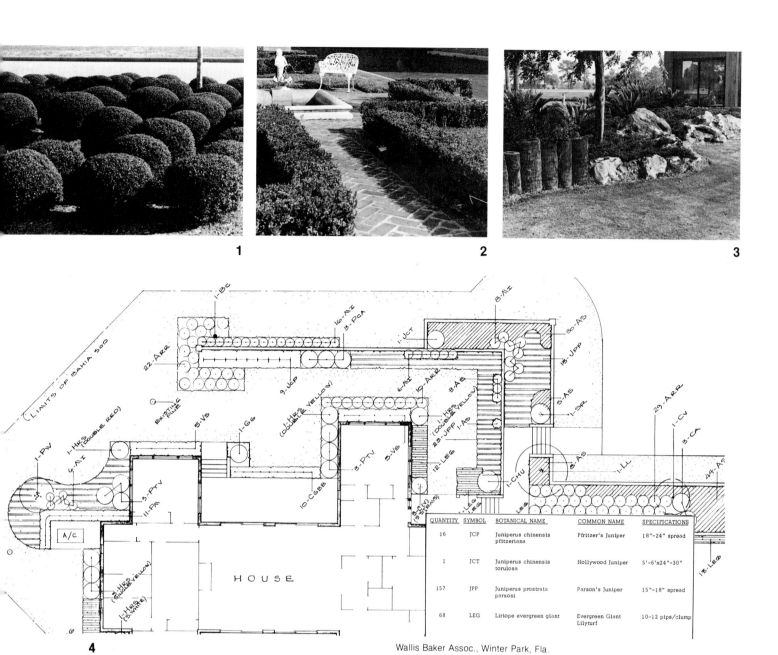

1　　　　　**2**　　　　　**3**

QUANTITY	SYMBOL	BOTANICAL NAME	COMMON NAME	SPECIFICATIONS
16	JCP	Juniperus chinensis pfitzeriana	Pfritzer's Juniper	18"-24" spread
1	JCT	Juniperus chinensis torulosa	Hollywood Juniper	5'-6'x24"-30"
157	JPP	Juniperus prostrata parsoni	Parson's Juniper	15"-18" spread
68	LEG	Liriope evergreen giant	Evergreen Giant Lilyturf	10-12 pips/clump

4　　　　　Wallis Baker Assoc., Winter Park, Fla.

landscaping

For some time after I got into this business, I'd regard the rendering as virtually completed when I'd finished putting in the building. My approach to the landscaping was to just slap in a few bushes and get it over with. Then I went through the process of home-shopping and had my attitude thankfully changed. I came to appreciate the extent to which the appearance of a building, no matter how attractive, depends on an effective landscaping scheme.

Landscape themes generally follow one of two themes. The formal type with trimmed privet hedges, holly, boxwood etc., **1** and **2,** or those having an informal free-flowing natural look, with low maintenance ground covers and self-sculptured shrubs, **3.**

The function of landscaping is to beautify the building, it shouldn't compete for interest with it. Sometimes the delineator is given license to put in whatever looks

good in the picture. Other times, a plan designed by a landscape architect has to be followed, **4,** requiring considerable research.

There's a temptation to skimp on landscaping and reduce it to a few symbols. But a developer's brochure very often shows two or three dozen homes, with variety being a significant selling point. His efforts can be negated if entourage is handled repetitiously throughout. Try to inject some individuality and have some fun with it. Get into the habit of 'seeing' landscape schemes as you drive around, keep a reference file on the subject. You'll know you're getting there when clients start passing your renderings on to the landscape architect for him to follow.

The examples above illustrate the stages of starting with the middle values and modeling with darker and lighter ones. I've always felt that the foreground of a landscape painting should have an inviting soft quality, so that the viewer would have no qualms about walking into the scene with bare feet. For this reason, I avoid intimidating spiky things in the immediate foreground and use materials like the ones above. More landscape treatments appear in the gallery chapter.

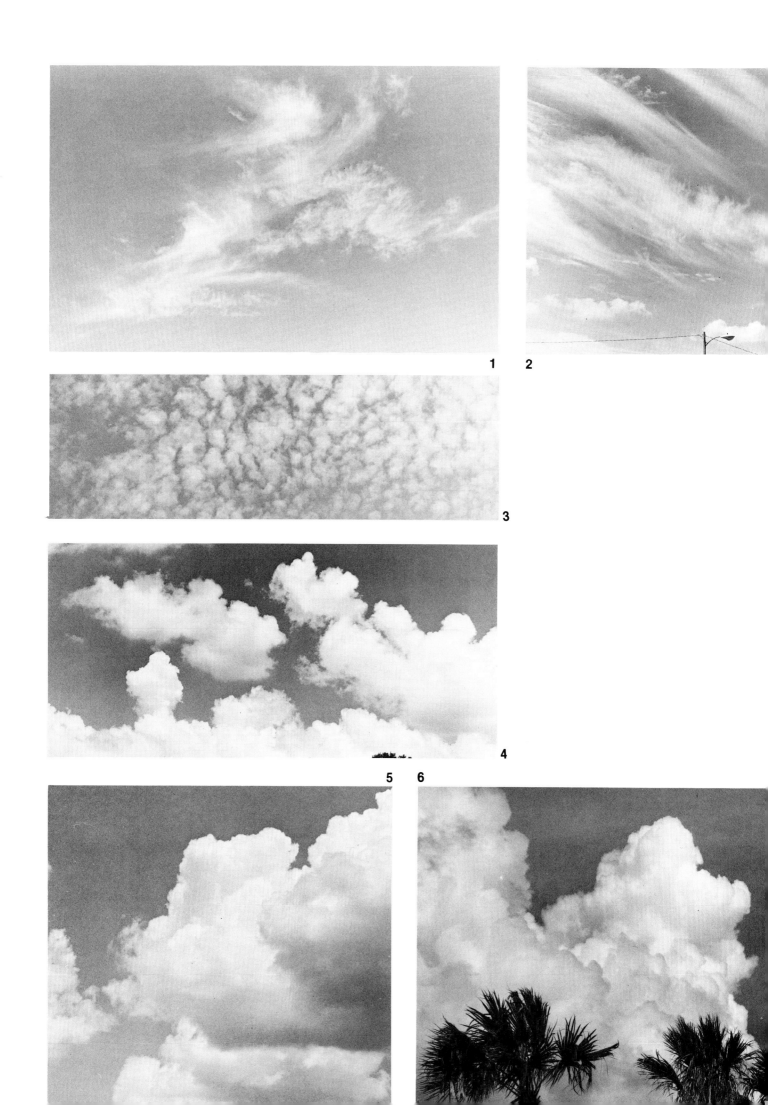

1 2 3 4 5 6

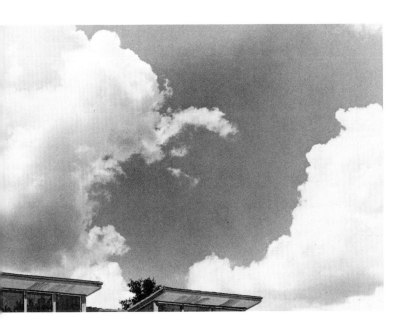

skies, clouds

The sky in a rendering usually accounts for a pretty big slice of the total picture area and deserves more than the passing attention it often gets. It's value as a backdrop to a building shouldn't be underrated, ask any architectural photographer. But so often you see renderings utterly botched because the vast area of sky has been handled sloppily, with clouds having no resemblence to anything that's ever been seen on this planet. Really, there's no excuse. The sky is there all the time, just waiting to be observed.

No other element determines the mood of a landscape more than sky. But unlike the landscape painter who has to be conversant with a whole range of cloud types to create many moods, our mood requirements are pre-set. We need only to concentrate on the one or two types that are consistent with fair, sunny conditions.

There are four basic cloud shapes known by Latin names that describe their appearance. "Cirrus", meaning wispy or curl—"cumulus" meaning heap or mass—"stratus" meaning spreading out, and "nimbus" meaning rain cloud. They're also described by altitude levels like 'alto' for middle altitude—above 8,000 feet, and by combinations like cumulo-nimbus.

The types I most often use are pictured at left. Cirrus, **1** and **2,** consist of tiny particles of ice and appear at high altitudes, above 20,000 feet. The other photos show the various forms taken by cumulus. From the pattern of alto-cumulus, **3,** then lower altitude cumulus in fragmented puffs, **4,** to denser and more organized masses with flat bases, **5.** Cumulus are the ones that build up into cumulo-nimbus, those colossal thunderheads, **6.**

Recognize that clouds have form and perspective (oh no, not that again?). Don't be baffled by their complexities, select the essential features and simplify. Use the arrangement of their shapes together with those of the sky between them in the overall composition scheme—as an 'optical path' for instance as illustrated above.

Take advantage of the fact that the sky is the first part of the rendering to be painted. With no time yet invested, we can afford to have a fling and indulge in the luxury of experimentation.

cirrus

These high altitude clouds are usually associated with the crisp early hours. I often employ their oblique windblown sweeps to dramatize roof lines or to animate an otherwise static composition.

First take a fully loaded 1″ flat brush and paint the graduated background sky, starting with general color and working with quick back and forth horizontal strokes. Now proceed down the board, adding progressively more white to the color. The secret of smooth blending here is to keep the paint very wet but still opaque, and working with rapid strokes. The value is lightened until it's almost white at the tree and building line.

Now the whole thing is left to dry, while I con my wife out of her can of spray starch. She buys the explanation that it now qualifies as tax deductible, and allows me to spray a light film of it over my sky. While this is still wet the clouds are put in, using an old brush and thinly diluted white. The character of the feathery wisps is created by *pushing* the brush and twisting it at the ends of the strokes.

Making the streaks narrower and closer together as they recede towards the horizon gives depth to the picture.

The reason for the raid on the laundry is that starch retards the rate of spread when painting wet-on-wet. The technique results in a filmy quality and natural looking edges that I wouldn't even attempt to reproduce with opaque pigment.

cumulus

1

2

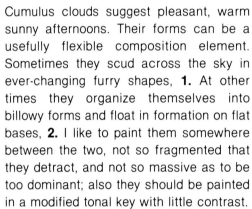

Cumulus clouds suggest pleasant, warm sunny afternoons. Their forms can be a usefully flexible composition element. Sometimes they scud across the sky in ever-changing furry shapes, **1.** At other times they organize themselves into billowy forms and float in formation on flat bases, **2.** I like to paint them somewhere between the two, not so fragmented that they detract, and not so massive as to be too dominant; also they should be painted in a modified tonal key with little contrast.

My method is to start with a graduated background as in the previous demonstration, then block in the cloud shapes. The best way to achieve the kind of shapes desired is by painting with a well-loaded brush, using a value midway between the two extremes of the background, then model the forms with lighter values. Paint the shapes smaller and closer together as they recede to indicate their perspective and give depth. The little woolly guys are scumbled in lightly with almost dry paint on the end of a finger. When getting down to the lightest value at the tree level, apply the paint thickly. This provides a rough surface that lends itself to the foliage texture which will be put in next.

Clouds shouldn't look as if they've been cut out and pasted on, try for a soft natural feel at the edges. If you have trouble studying actual clouds, you might find picture post-cards a useful source of reference. I use them a lot.

shadows

1

2

The points discussed in chapter 3 regarding the part played by shadows in expressing form, also apply to the general surroundings in a rendering. At **1,** tree shadows are used to express the forms of the earth berms, eliminating the need for a whole lot of modeling.

Heavy foreground shadows help to frame the subject and round-off distracting corners of the picture. The tree shadows at **2** and **3** serve a two-fold purpose. Besides suggesting trees that are out of view behind us, they're arranged so that the eye is lead into the picture. It sometimes happens that an architectural element such as the entrance, which would normally be a focal point, is hidden. By using shadows in the way shown at **2,** the eye is lead in the desired direction. At **3,** the 'S' shaped open area forms an 'optical path' into the picture. To get a dappled sunlight effect, put the shadows in solid then paint the lighted areas in full, rounded shapes.

In the bottom illustration, the subordinate elements of a foreground have been handled in a very low key with little tonal difference between planes, leaving their form to be suggested mainly by shadows.

3

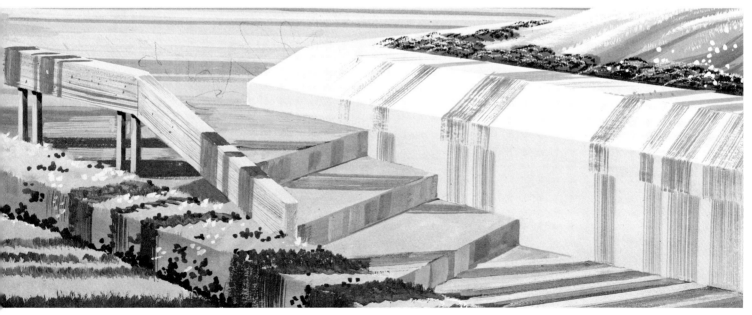

water

You'll not often be called upon to render water in a single-family residence application. However, it's use is becoming more frequent in multi-family unit situations as developers are being required to make provision for water retention.

Like clouds, its constant state of movement can make it difficult to study, you may find it easier working with photographs. I used the slide at **1** for the rendering here, **2.**

The complexities of water are similar to those of glass we dealt with earlier. The same approach applies — eliminate all but the essentials. Stay away from the 'black lagoon' type of water. It doesn't read well in renderings, even photographers have trouble with it. Paint it as a reflection of the general sky color. We obviously rely on reflections to say 'wet', but limit them to those of the more prominent elements close to the water's edge.

Starting with the lighter value at the top, the darker values are blended in as I work downwards to the foreground. I work with the paint pretty thin in order to retain the nature of the board's surface for subsequent stages.

The reflections are added using a square ended brush against a ruler. The tapering off effect is produced by lifting the brush as I stroke quickly down.

Again using the ruler, I then put in the streaks of white, indicating ruffled water. These strokes are made by dragging an almost dry brush lightly across the grain to get a shimmering effect. They also serve to express the receding horizontal plane.

Finally, a few wave 'symbols' are added to the foreground in light and dark values.

1

2

PEOPLE/WALKING

PEOPLE/BEACH

CARS

MATADOR SEDAN

props

Besides the obvious ones of people and cars, the props in a rendering can be anything that contributes to the story-telling process. While not normally included in renderings of single-family residences unless specifically requested, in renderings of commercial subjects they're an essential component. They provide a feeling of scale, atmosphere and help explain the function of the building.

The presence of aspects not actually shown in the rendering, but which are related to the building's function can be indicated in a variety of ways. For instance, the proximity of an airport to a hotel or car rental agency can be conveyed by showing airplanes taking off and landing in the background. In the apartment field, a whole range of props can be incorporated to indicate various life styles. To this end, the delineator should be thoroughly familiar with the client's selling points. Amenities he's offering such as golf, fishing, tennis etc., can be suggested with golf carts, boats, and people dressed for these activities.

Any particular sales orientation should also be determined. This may be towards young people attending a nearby college (suggesting hot-rods, dune buggies etc.), or executive level people (suggesting imported hot-rods). The community may be adult only, or exclusively for retirees. Determining all pertinent factors before starting the job will allow you to get into the part, as it were, and incorporate them in a natural way rather than as an afterthought. I remember one of my pencil renderings coming back for a change. I'd drawn a lady prominently in the foreground walking hand in hand with her young daughter. It turned out the apartments were adult only, but pets were allowed. After substituting a dog in the place of the girl, the rendering came back again — only small dogs were allowed. I suppose you let your pup reach a certain size then either stunt his growth or train him to walk on his knees.

Unless you are one of those enviably talented artists that can draw figures well, you're going to require good source material. The benefits of building up reference files just cannot be overemphasized. Make a daily habit of clipping from anything you can get your hands on. Take your own photographs of people. If you're not comfortable with the reaction of some people to this, try an area like an amusement park where a camera is less conspicuous.

The scrap from my files, opposite, include fashion ads (with acknowledgements to the artists), poses purchased from a reference service, small pictures clipped from travel brochures and pasted to cards by my daughter for a nickel a sheet, vacation snapshots, and the family acting as decoys while I shoot passers-by.

Pictures of practically every automobile on the road can be found in the manufacturer's brochures. Depending on your adeptness at fending off salesmen, you can track down all of them on a lunch break.

The effectiveness of any files depends on ease of retrieval. When files get so bulky that searching becomes a chore, subdivide the categories into 'people/walking'—'people/beach' etc.

people

It's not essential that photographs of figures fit your requirements exactly. The camera freezes even walking action in some awkward looking positions or poses that don't reflect the action desired. Most any picture can be used as a basis and changed to suit a different mood or even re-clothed into another generation, **1**.

Good animation should have a fluid feel that suggests before and after positions. A good way to study walking figures is to position yourself with a sketchpad where you can look out onto a street. Focus on a person walking then 'freeze' the action by snapping your eyes shut. That last image will remain long enough for you to then dash off a quick sketch.

De-emphasize feet, they tend to anchor the figure too solidly to the ground. Make your figures attractive, not glamorous necessarily but smartly and appropriately attired—not too kinky.

The examples at **2** and **3** are about the size of figures in the average street scene rendering. Note how light and dark values added to the same silhouette produces different poses. All the figures were first blocked in as mid-tone silhouettes then modelled with a few strokes of light and dark values. Two or three for the smaller figures, **2**. A few more for those in the foreground, **3**.

Direct your 'extras' so that their actions are consistent with the particular mood being created. The angles of striding limbs suggests excitement and purposefulness not necessarily serious, **4**. Softer

1

2

4

5

lines suggest a relaxed strolling mood consistent with leisure activities and contentment, **5**. Some scenes call for a mixture of emotions. Shopping for instance can be a frantic hustle for some, a pleasant saunter for others.

One key to realistic posture I find, lies in the line across the shoulders. The shoulder on the side supporting the body's weight is often lower than the other.

The procedure of plotting figures in an eye-level view on level ground, is simply a matter of placing the eyes roughly in line with the horizon line, **6**. The figures here are traced from the pictures on page 86. Their position within the picture is determined by their size and where the feet happen to fall. This is a plaza type situation. When pedestrian traffic is directional, figure placement is more critical.

When the eye-level is elevated, figures have to fit between lines of perspective converging to vanishing points on the horizon line, **7**.

6

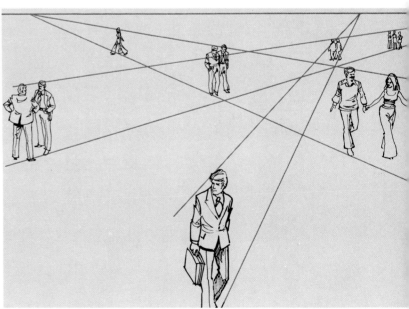

3 **7**

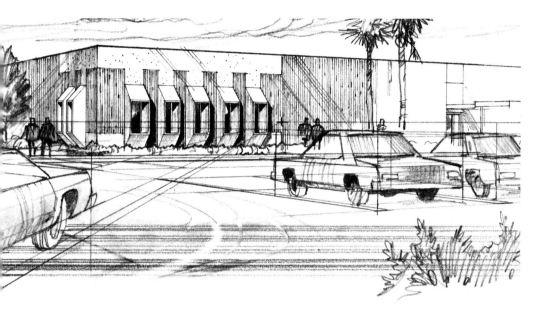

cars

As with people, the inclusion of cars in a rendering is essential for realism. They should be executed in the same style as the rest of the rendering and not skimped over for lack of observation.

The dimensions **1**, give or take a few inches, apply to most cars in this mid-size range. Correct proportions are essential if realism is to be achieved.

Cars should be plotted in proper perspective along with the building, **2**. One way is to apply dry-transfer scale cars to the site plan **3**.

A characteristic of cars that we have going for us when depicting them in line or tone, is the fact that chrome strips and the joints between panels provide built in outlines. These automatically suggest form **4**.

Painting cars in casein can be broken down into three basic stages. At **5**, the basic forms were established in mid-values using a square ended brush. Modelling was then done with lighter and darker values. Like all glossy materials, upper and lower surfaces are not neces-

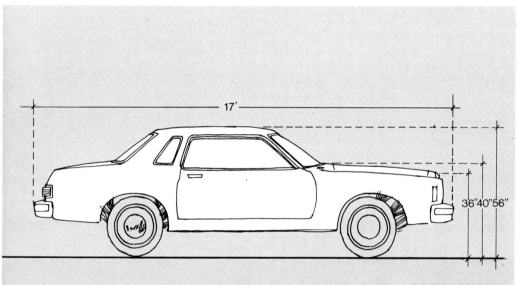

17'

36"40"56"

1

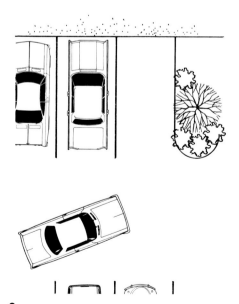

2   **3**

sarily the lightest and darkest. The top of the hood picks up reflections from the windshield, trees, etc., and the lower door panels reflect the sunlit ground. In the final stages a pointed brush was used to paint the darker lines, chrome strips and highlights.

When painting chrome, bear in mind that it consists of a subdued reflection of its surrounding. Bumpers reflect mostly road color, keep sky color to a minimum. When working from brochure pictures allow for the fact that these are airbrushed to showroom brilliance. Tone down the sparkle or they'll loom out of the picture.

When adding cars to a bird's-eye view, **6**. we're working to a much smaller scale and painting lots of them. (I've put as many as fourteen hundred in one rendering). Realism requires these numbers. Ten cars in front of a 600 unit condominium complex just doesn't make it. They necessarily have to be simplified to three or four brush strokes.

This is the procedure I used in adding the cars and people to the rendering reproduced on pages 128-129.

5

4

6

Some figures and cars had been roughly indicated on the perspective block-out for purposes of scale. The possibility of rejection in favor of a different view didn't warrant a time-consuming search through files for anything more definite at this stage. I'd formed some thoughts on people types while rendering the building and background. A search through the files turned up pictures that fitted the requirements of people types, pedestrian and traffic flow, **1**. I like to weave a story around the characters — the businessman has just secured a loan, the young marrieds have just made their final car payment, the young girl has opened her first savings account.

A sheet of acetate was now taped over the rendering. This allowed me to try out various arrangements, sizes and overlappings (for depth and distance). I also used this stage to judge the effect of different colors, **2**. Next I drew the props in detail on tracing paper placed over the perspective, **3**. The detail at **4** is reproduced at same size.

1

4

the rendering

Come now into the studio and visit awhile. We'll discuss materials, tools and equipment then you can look over my shoulder while I paint a casein rendering.

Casein belongs to the group of water soluble paints generally known as tempera. I don't feel it enjoys the popularity it deserves, I've come across art supply stores who've never even heard of it. This is a pity because it possesses unique qualities that I'm sure many artists would appreciate. The vehicle used to bind the pigment together is a derivative of milk. This makes for a working consistency that is congenially smooth with far less of the 'brush drag' associated with gummier mediums.

It's this consistency that helps produce the crisp, sharp edges essential for precise delineation and also allows those essential fine lines to be drawn with a ruling pen.

Like acrylics, casein can be used transparently as well as opaquely and has a quick convenient drying time. When using casein transparently, an area of wash will 'set up' enough to allow a second wash to be laid over it almost immediately without disturbing the underpainting. Adding a few drops of Casein Emulsion to the water improves the film integrity and makes the paint flow even more smoothly.

Sometimes I use acrylic paints for certain effects. One of its characteristics I use to advantage is the way brush marks are accentuated when acrylic is extended with Matte Medium. I use this to achieve the texture of large tree masses in aerial views. Another way in which I find this feature useful is when painting a quickie type of rendering. Before putting in the trees, the background is covered with a coat of Gloss Medium. The way in which this slick surface emphasizes every brush mark then allows a reasonable bark and foliage texture to be suggested with a minimum of strokes.

Casein can be pretty hard on brushes so you need the best sable ones. I've found actual brush manipulation to be as personal as handwriting, what works for one artist doesn't for another, so by all means experiment with different types.

The brushes shown opposite are the ones that work for me: **1**, Delta 5000 No. 3 —pointed. **2**, Delta 1107 No. 12—pointed but worn to a rounded end. **3**, **4** and **5**, Grumbacher 9355 No's 4, 6, 11—square ended. **6**, Grumbacher 4116 3/8″—flat. **7**, Delta 5000 No. 2—pointed. **8**, Grumbacher Aquarelle 1″—flat. **9**, Delta 502 No. 8—worn pointed. Other items shown are **10**, Ruling pen. **11**, Stipple brush for splatter effects of gravel etc. **12**, Steel stylus for transferring the perspective to the illustration board through a sheet of graphite paper.

For what it's worth, the little nook opposite is my rendering mill. On the shelf at my left are my reference files in vertical racks. In front of the drawing board are

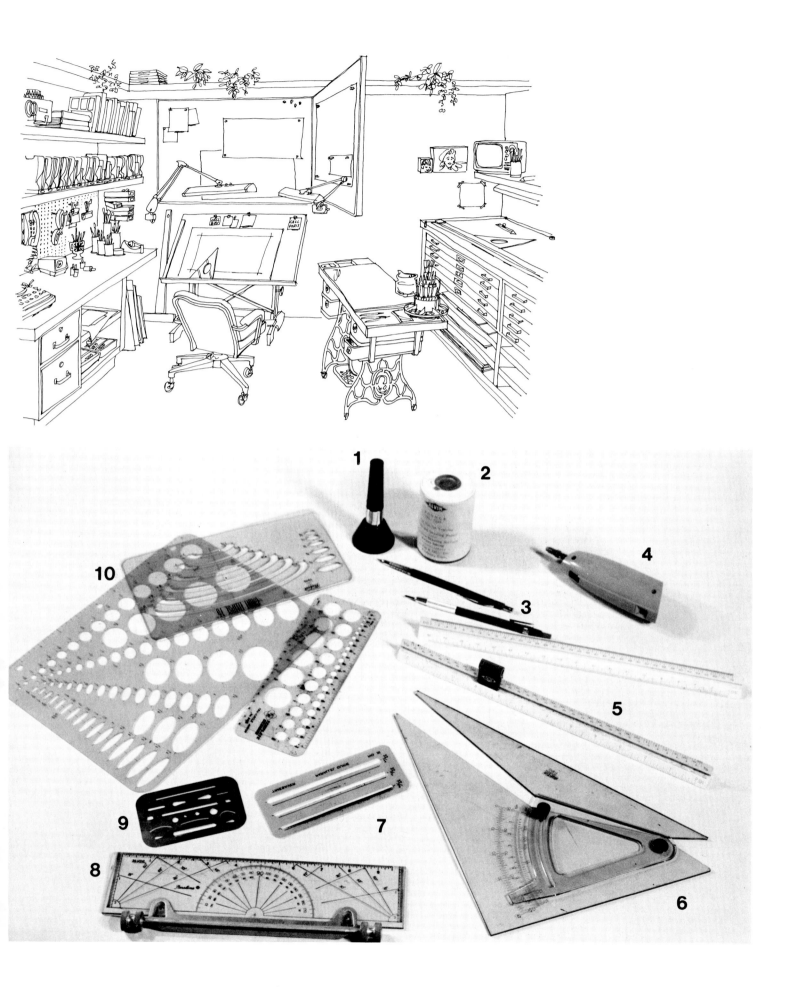

two tack boards for holding blueprints of the job being worked on. The one on the right is hinged, allowing it to be used while working at the perspective table on the extreme right and also double as a screen for the slide projector positioned on the shelf far left. The taboret is an old sewing machine rescued from a farmer's barn. I adapted the top to hold a sheet of plate glass for a palette. I clean this by scraping the paint through a hole at the end into a bin fixed beneath.

Opposite bottom, are the various tools I use at the perspective board. **1**, pencil pointer. **2**, Pounce powder for degreasing the paper surface before drawing in ink. **3**, lead holders. **4**, electric eraser. **5**, engineers and architects scale rules. **6**, adjustable triangle. **7**, parallel guide. **8**, parallel rule. **9**, erasing shield. **10**, various circle and ellipse templates.

It's always an advantage to visit the site if possible. A strip of Polaroid shots taken from the same station point as the rendering is of great help back at the studio. It's often important that specific existing trees be shown on the final rendering. If a plan on which trees have been plotted is not available, a pocket optical rangefinder is a useful gadget to carry around. With this you can accurately measure distances between anything that will appear in the rendering and with a bit of simple geometry calculate heights of trees and surrounding structures.

Allow for the fact that existing trees will probably be trimmed at the behest of the landscape architects, as was the case with the before and after photos below.

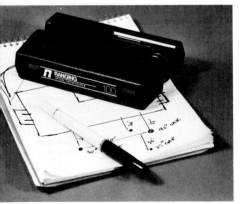

composition

If there's one thing that's been demonstrated by artists in recent years, it's that the traditional 'golden rules' of composition can be successfully breached. We're now thinking more in terms of basic abstract pattern —and almost anything goes.

The composition of architectural renderings is confined within a narrow set of precepts, dictated by the requirement that the building is the main attraction. Other units are also decided for us. Existing buildings and specified plantings like a row of trees on 30' centers all serve to reduce our options.

I feel that this conditioning to the abstract has freed us from inhibiting cliches like 'graphic weight' and 'optical fulcrum.' As long as we avoid obvious pitfalls like those opposite, recognize a feature such as an entrance as a focal point and provide optical paths into the picture, we can concentrate on arranging the elements so that they display the client's product to best advantage.

The composition roughs here were done on blueprints of the perspective on page 21. I like to make at least two of these to explore various possibilities.

The files turned up a set of photographs and pages from an old sketch book of tree types that fitted the situation.

1

2 **3**

no no's

Having said anything goes, here are some obvious exceptions:

1 — Tree outlines following roof lines.

2 — Cloud shapes following tree shapes. Echoing shapes within a picture is an old landscape painters' device and happens in the patterns of nature. But it shouldn't be this blatant.

3 — Tree trunks clashing with architectural elements.

4 — Trees spaced too symmetrically.

5 — Lines of surrounding elements clashing with angles of the building or each other, causing tension spots.

6 — Trees out of scale. A common mistake of beginners when copying from pictures without understanding tree types.

Amidst the haste of meeting a deadline, all these dumb things can occur, (you'll probably find a few in this book). The possibilities are reduced however, by taking the time to make a rough layout.

4

5

6

My palette is comprised of
Cadmium Yellow, Cadmium Red, Alizarin
Crimson, Light Red, Burnt Sienna,
Raw Umber, Cadmium Green, Paynes Grey,
Phthalo Green, Cerulean Blue, Ivory
Black and Titanium White.

Tempera painting requires a board
with a tooth. I use Crescent No. 100.
The perspective is transferred to it
by placing a sheet of engineer's
graphite underneath, then tracing the
outlines with a steel stylus using
T-square and triangle.

1. The sky is painted in the manner
described on page 82. I use the 1″
flat Aquarelle brush and a mixture
of Cerulean Blue, Phthalo Green and
White. Distant trees are painted
with Phthalo Green and White.

2. The darkest values of the tree
foliage are added with various
mixtures of greens. Dark for the large
oaks and viburnum hedge, light for
the young trees and bluish for the
evergreens. I paint with a pushing
stroke to get a broken outline.

3. Next I paint the tree trunks and branches in their mid-value with a number 3 pointed brush. Don't make the mistake of painting tree bark too brown, it's really a warm grey.

4. I now model some of the branches, first with the darker then with lighter warm grey values. The young trees are painted lighter and smoother textured than the older ones. Some of the branches are going to be covered up by the next step, so modelling at this stage is more a matter of establishing light against dark and vice versa.

5. Here I model the tree foliage with progressively lighter values of the various greens. I then go back and finish modelling the trunks and branches.

Note that up until now I've been working from the distance towards the foreground as far as the house. That will be next, but first, the white board in the foreground needs to be eliminated to prevent it influencing the tonal values.

6. I usually leave foreground trees till last. But as this one doesn't conflict with any unpainted areas and is such a dominant feature, I put it in now. Next I paint the base color of the roof, then indicate the shingles with a small pointed brush along a ruler.

As I get into painting the materials, I dab patches of their colors in the margins. This helps me later to judge the effect of colors that fall next to them.

7. I finish the roof by adding the highlights with a small square-ended brush. I'm going to have to use a ruling pen on the window mullions so the windows are put in next to give them time to dry hard.

The wood areas of chimney, garage and front doors are next, followed by the base coat of the stone panels —painted thickly in a mid-value.

8. The stone panels are modelled, first with darker values, then the highlights. Door panels are indicated with brush and ruler. Back to the windows to rule in the mullions.

Whenever the ruling pen is to be used, paint that area before the one adjacent to it if possible. This will allow you to zip right through and thus avoid the blob of paint that occurs when you stop to lift the pen from the surface. I now move to the stucco walls, starting with the darker shade.

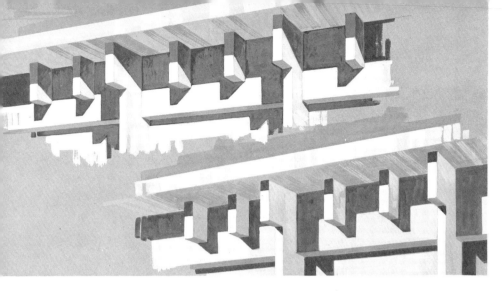

9. When the direction of light is angled to illuminate both front and side planes, the difference in their values can be pretty subtle. Because colors dry a slightly different color to when wet, it's advisable to make tests and record them in the margins before committing yourself.

I complete the stucco areas, then add the shadows of the roof overhangs.

To depict architectural forms realistically, you should observe the tonal effects of shadow, shade, and reflected light under different sun-angles. Just a couple of studied exercises like those above can teach you a lot.

10. Painting the wood tone of the trim at the eaves and around the walls completes the house. A dark colored overhang can sometimes be close in value to its shadow. In this case the two areas are conveniently separated by a strip of reflected light on the underside of the soffit.

11. After the path and drive are painted, the final stages are started by laying in the grass. I work towards the foreground with darkening gradations of Cadmium Green, Grey and White. The tree shadows are then dabbed in with a splayed-out flat brush. Next I paint the darker values of the various shrubbery greens, from the bright greens of the Asparagus Fern to the blue greys of the Juniper ground cover. The trunks and branches of the Crape Myrtle at far left are put in and modelled.

12. Finally, the plantings are modelled with dark, then light values. The immediate foreground shrubbery is painted darkest to give depth to the picture.

The final rendering is reproduced in color on page 113.

gallery

Most artists, consciously or otherwise, work in an individual style through which they become identified. When working in tempera I'm more or less locked into the kind of approach I've just demonstrated. Striving for realism pure and simple, is an on-going challenge I've yet to find monotonous for very long. The same would apply were I to specialize in other full tonal mediums such as pencil or watercolor.

There's a lot to be said however, for being in a position to offer clients a choice. I find using various pen and ink techniques to be a convenient way of achieving this.

For some years I drew cartoons for an agency in Switzerland who syndicated them world-wide. It didn't take me long to realize that sales potential was limited by two factors; 1, different editors preferred different styles of drawing, and 2, any editor would consider only so many cartoons drawn by one artist regardless of quality. I was soon drawing in four styles under four pen-names. I found I had to fight monotony less and that each style benefited immeasurably. I also started using up more bank deposit slips.

I think that's good business; I still use the same approach and find it an advantage in these types of situations:

One style may have become identifed with a certain builder — his competitor requests a different approach.

Two or three architect clients may be entered in the same competition for a job — you can draw each one in a different style to maintain individuality.

Art directors are constantly on the lookout for new angles — you can create a style tailored to a particular theme.

There are many ways to go in all media. We'll be talking about a few approaches, some dictated by the client's requirements, others by the type of subject.

In the rendering opposite, I wanted to convey the feeling of Mr. Solomon's backyard — this gorgeous beach and the Gulf of Mexico. The expanse of dazzling white sand was suggested by stretching the cone of vision in the foreground. The sea-grapes were incorporated to establish 'bottom edge'. The feeling of brilliant tropical sunshine was heightened throughout by losing outlines wherever possible and still retaining shape and structure.

Building up the tones of the Casuarina trees and dune grass with many fine lines, gave them a softness that contrasted with the bold lines of the architecture. The cast shadows on the building were kept in a luminous high key to give the effect of so much light reflected off the beach.

As with other pen and ink drawings throughout the book, the pens used were the capillary-type technical fountain pens. I use both the Koh-i-noor Rapidograph and the Castell TG.

The greatest difference between working with paint and drawing with a linear medium, is probably the physical one of laying down areas of tone and texture. With pure pen and ink there are no short-cuts, you've just got to get in there and make lots of marks. Depicting tonal values of building materials is best done by using triangles and T-square. Different values being obtained by crosshatching at varying angles, varying the spacing between lines and using different pen thicknesses. The values of other textures are best built up with various free-hand strokes.

Mr. Syd Solomon residence. Architect: Gene Leedy, Winter Haven, Florida

Mr. Don Ruckman residence. Architect: DeWitt Bruen MacLean, Jacksonville, Florida

Architect: Bob Koch, AIA, Orlando, Florida

Here are three different approaches to the same type of subject—the heavily wooded site.

The foliage in the rendering at left was done with the same basic pattern of strokes throughout. Different values were built up by varying degrees of overlapping and with different size pens. The shadows on the building were filled in solid to give the house more contrast and prevent it blending too much with the background.

The other two examples illustrate short-cut alternatives to indicating large areas of foliage. The one at far left was made specifically for reproduction in a brochure. The foliage masses were drawn in simple outline and a mechanical half-tone screen added during the printing stage. This had the effect of giving tonal weight and concentrating maximum contrast on the house.

The technique used in the other drawing is a combination of line and dry-transfer textures—the kind you rub down. The building was rendered first. Then patterns representing foliage, wood, stone and grass were applied using sheets of Letraset Instantex and Geoex.

Matsche Construction Co., Eustis, Florida

The medium used for tonal values here was Zipatone Shading Films. These are sheets of thin acetate that have half-tone screens and patterns printed on the front side and an adhesive coating on the back.

The half-tone screen type was used here to simulate regular half-tone printing. Two kinds were used—Coordinated Screen Tints which range in values from 10% to 80% and Graduated Screen Tints. The latter are graduated from 10% to 90% across the same sheet and were used here on the tree trunks.

A piece of film slightly larger than the area to be shaded is placed on the artwork. The excess film is then trimmed away with the point of a sharp knife and the remaining film burnished down firmly. The printing being on top allows finer details and highlights to be scratched off.

Avoid having the angle of the screen grid at or close to 90° or the dot pattern will be apparent. Also, overlapping the screens can cause 'screen clash' (a plaid pattern). To avoid this, rotate the top film back and forth to find the angle at which this moire effect disappears.

Zipatone also puts out Perspective Sheets. These are printed with fine lines that diminish to a vanishing point and are available in a range of different line spacings.

Architect: Tom Price, Winter Park, Florida

The Frazier Group, Merrifield, Virginia

A bit of whimsey. A series of renderings done in this kind of decorative treatment makes for good eye appeal in a brochure format. It's really just a rendered elevation. Except for the roof, steps and driveway, the house was traced directly from the architect's drawing. The style wouldn't be appropriate for every subject, but it was felt this storybook type of house and its texture lent themselves to it.

Some useful extra mileage can be gotten from line renderings by coloring a Mylar print of the original, opposite. The color was added by using acrylics applied to the reverse side of the Mylar. Painting was done in reverse of the normal procedure i.e. painting the foreground elements first then painting the background over them, left. The client is left with a set of pictures to pretty up his sales office and the original line drawings to use for reproduction.

Subject of the earlier demonstration. Baywood Design & Construction, Winter Park, Florida

Ashington-Pickett Construction Co. Inc., Orlando, Florida

vignettes

The vignette is less formal than an 'edge-to-edge' treatment. It focuses attention on to the subject, particularly when colored boards are used. It's a most attractive format.

When drawing in black and white with pen and ink or pencil, we tend to think in vignette terms quite naturally as the white of the background automatically carries throughout the picture. The same principle applies when working on colored board by retaining the background color in portions of the picture, or by using a board whose color harmonizes with the subject.

The rendering at left was painted with

Hailey Smith — Designer, Maitland, Florida

casein on Crescent Tampico Brown board. The other was drawn with 2B and 4B pencils on Crescent Congo Green, then colored with a combination of thin casein washes and Eagle Prismacolor pencils.

Areas of transition between the work and background color were handled in various ways. They included thinning the paint to a wash at the edges, dry brush strokes, and by the arrangement of foliage shapes.

When painting on colored boards, I find color mixing is easier if I replace the white board normally under my glass palette with a sheet the same color as the one on which I'm working.

W. McTammany, Del.

Wm. L. Canole residence. Architects: Rogers, Lovelock & Fritz, Winter Park, Florida

Frazier Group, Merrifield, Virginia

STANTON

watercolor

If I'd been halfway bright, any mention of watercolor would have preceded my pontificating about jumping from one medium to another.

To render well with pure transparent watercolor, (using no opaque color at all) really calls for specialized skills.

As is evident by the rendering at left, Wallace McTammany is such a specialist. His authorative handling of tonal values and entourage achieves superb realism. Following the practice essential when working with watercolor, Mr. McTammany uses preliminary 'value studies'. He does these meticulously in charcoal and pencil on thin tracing paper laid over the perspective layout. The final painting is done on Strathmore illustration board.

For my effort, bottom left, I used D'Arches rough paper. The roughness precludes any attempt at fine detail but I find it fun to handle a traditional subject like this with traditional watercolor technique. As the same-size detail shows, the rough surface lends itself to the vibrant effect of bright sunlight on brick, grass and foliage.

The example below was painted as an 'on the spot' demonstration for a student group. It runs the gamut of standard watercolor tricks—wet-on-wet, rubber cement frisket, knife scratching, spatter etc.

Black and white sketch

Greater Construction Corp., Casselberry, Florida

1 Baywood Design & Construction Inc., Winter Park, Florida

2 Greater Construction Corp., Casselberry, Florida

3 Hailey Smith — Designer, Maitland, Florida

quickies

The most frequently asked for type. Usually at the least convenient time —naturally. But it should be possible to squeeze one into any schedule with little trouble. All the examples here were done inside 25 minutes after the perspective had been blocked out.

The choice of medium was dictated solely by the mood I happened to be in or whatever was handy at the time. If I've been working in pencil for six days straight, it's easier to stay with pencil than go through the mental gear-changing that switching to something else would require.

The tempera at **1** was painted on a piece of Crescent Stone Gray matt board. Most of it was done with a half inch flat brush, using a corner of it for branches etc.

For **2, 3** and **4,** color was added to black-line blueprints of the perspective block-outs. 2 was colored with Prismacolor pencils. For 3, felt-tip markers were used. The print for the rendering at **4** was dry-mounted to board and colored with acrylics. The color was applied pretty loosely then pulled together in the building by black lines drawn with a ruling pen.

In the example at right, a glossy photographic print was colored with felt-tip markers then sprayed with Krylon Acrylic Coating to achieve the texture. It is reproduced here at same size.

4 The McCarthy Company, Falls Church, Virginia

commercial

Variety! — Not the least agreeable bonus when rendering projects that fall in the category of commercial. The examples here — a ski-lodge in Colorado — an oil terminal in the Netherland Antilles — a pioneer theme shopping center — an office building in Saudi Arabia, were all done over a four week period. Not your typical month, granted, but they serve to illustrate the diversity of exciting challenges this profession can provide. Even with just a 'mom and pop' business like mine, operating from a small town.

Those of us from outside the architectural profession often get our first start in this business by making renderings of homes for a local builder/developer. The interests of most development companies however, are usually pretty diversified, and sooner or later we're asked to tackle a commercial project. It may be just a single story office building or a 500 unit apartment complex. But whatever it is, as we discussed earlier, in terms of basic fundamentals it's not as big a step as it may first appear to be. The differences are mainly ones of scale and function.

I'm not suggesting you plunge recklessly into something that may be way above your head. If you honestly feel a job is beyond your capabilities at that particular stage of your development, you'd be wise to level with your client

Omni Realty Corp., Jacksonville. Architects: Areneo, McCulley & Parker, Jacksonville, Florida

DSJ Developments Inc., Winter Park, Florida

Statia Terminals, N.V., Miami, Florida

Stevens & Walton, Architects, Orlando, Florida

rather than risk performing below his expectations. Recognize that you have a stake in his reputation too.

In cases where the project is a logical progression of your client's activities, the chances are that your progression can run parallel. The first commercial project I took on some years ago, was a 400 unit apartment complex for a client who, until then, had been involved only with houses. My initial attack of the terrors only diminished when I realized that it was just a case of rendering a large house, then repeating it 50 times. A reaction that, I was to find out later, happened to correspond with that of the client.

The types of assignments illustrated here can send you scurrying for reference pictures. A search through old Christmas cards from back home can turn up snow scenes, a friendly travel agent can supply pictures of foreign parts, and sitting through a late night Western can even prove profitable. It also pays of course to collect your own source material. Keep files on anything—clips from travel magazines, friends' vacation post cards etc. When taking vacation or business trips, make a point of photographing features that could be of value should you ever be called on to render a project in that area.

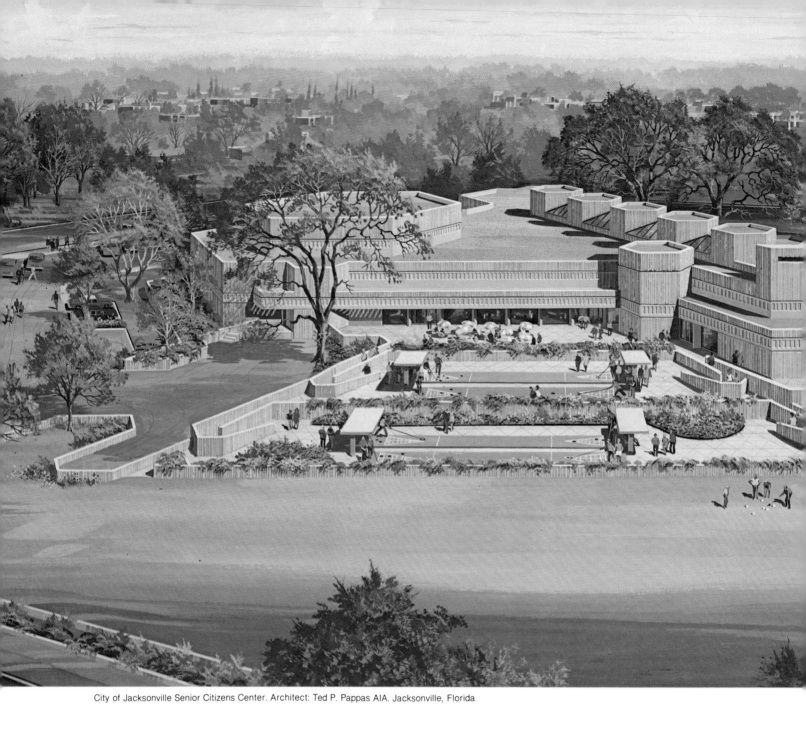

City of Jacksonville Senior Citizens Center. Architect: Ted P. Pappas AIA. Jacksonville, Florida

bird's-eye views

An aerial viewpoint is sometimes the only way of illustrating a project with a single picture. In the case of the Senior Citizens Center, the unusual plan and geometric elements would be obvious when actually approaching the building at ground level due to the many angles it would be seen from. A bird's-eye view tells the story in one shot and includes the surroundings on all sides.

Plotting the perspective was more simple than the plan might suggest. By positioning the plan with one side parallel to the picture plane, all lines for that side ran horizontally. Only two vanishing points were then required for the other angles. A third one was only needed for a few elements running perpendicular to the picture plane. Aerial views of this type shouldn't be from so high that too much emphasis is given to the roof at the expense of architectural elevation detail. Where overhangs are involved, a few exploratory rough drafts may be required to find a happy medium.

The relationship to existing trees had been a significant consideration in the design of the building and its placement on the site. Each tree therefore had to be located and depicted accurately, calling for visits to the site and numerous photos.

For the Okeeheelee Park rendering, the photo method was ideal for plotting the free-forms in correct perspective. When painting the background, progressively cooler colors were used towards the horizon and field shapes diminished to a vanishing point to create the illusions of distance and establish the horizontal plane.

The use of cloud shadows in aerial views adds realism and suggests movement. In this example, I exploited the tonal interplay between areas of cloud shadows and sunlit patches to highlight certain areas. With composition devices like tree trunks and overhangs obviously not a factor in aerials, cloud shadows can be usefully employed across the foreground to frame the subject and give depth to the picture.

An elevated viewpoint naturally exposes a considerable amount of surrounding area. Background elements are brought into view that are often important to the story and may even be the reason for a bird's-eye view being specified. Features such as highways, airports, schools, lakes and rivers sometimes several miles away, have to be shown in some detail and located in correct relationship. For ultimate accuracy of course, nothing beats photographing the area yourself from the air if the budget allows.

Okeeheelee State Park.
Gee & Jenson, Engineers-Architects-Planners, Inc.
West Palm Beach, Florida

123

College of Education Complex, Florida Tech. University. Architects: Lemon & Megginson AIA., Titusville, Florida

124

Rosemont Office Building, MGIC-Janis Properties, Miami, Florida. Architects: Tom Price/Don Duer, Winter Park, Florida

Same size detail.

The FTU building is another example of an aerial view dictated by the design of the building. I was fortunate in this case to have access to a study model made by the architect. This allowed me to photograph it from many angles —then use the one showing the building to its best advantage to construct the perspective on. This view was selected because it is high enough for the configuration of the building to be conveyed by the roof lines, and low enough to relate to from ground level. Flat-land architects, unlike their counterparts in the hills, don't have to concern themselves with roofs being visible. There would normally be a lot of junk up there in the way of air-conditioning equipment etc. So we lie a little.

Painting the building presented a bit of a challenge. The bricks face seven different angles and for good measure are laid in ribbons of English Bond alternating with Running Bond. Several tests were made to work out the most effective sun angle.

Angles were also a feature to be reckoned with in the prow shaped Rosemont building. The structure here was of sufficient height for the angles to read from a ground level viewpoint. A little license was taken with the position of the handrails so that they echoed the angles of the architecture and formed an S shape visual path into the entrance.

125

night scenes

Illustrating public buildings whose function is night-time oriented obviously calls for night scenes.

With the buildings for the most part cloaked in darkness, a night scene is usually more of a mood illustration than a delineation of the architecture. The Auditorium rendering offered an opportunity to attempt both.

The project was a controversial renovation of the existing structure, so the presentation required the architectural additions to be spelled out as they would be in a normal daylight setting. The most unique feature though, the preservation of the old classic-revival facade inside a tinted glass shell, would be only visible from the street when illuminated by the lobby lights.

It was decided that both conditions would exist just before sundown. A time that also conveniently justified the story-telling aspect of the elegant audience arriving for an evening symphony performance.

For the perspective of the Church Street Station rendering (another renovation project) I used slides taken from an adjacent hi-rise building.

The camera was also used for the Music Hall rendering. Without it, drawing the elaborate 'art deco' graphics in perspective would have been pretty tedious. The marquee elements were cut out of foam-core board and attached to the architect's elevation drawing. This simple model was then taped to a wall outside and photographed from the desired viewpoint. In the final rendering, the brightly lit areas were painted with transparent washes of acrylic color for maximum brilliance.

When painting daylight renderings innumerable consistencies have to be adhered to in order to cater to peoples' perception of realism—direction of light—shadows—color—materials—distance etc. Night-time releases us from most of these limitations and consequently allows far more freedom of expression. Shadows can be thrown in any direction, colors manipulated for any effect and desired details vividly highlighted while losing others in mysterious darkness.

One thing regarding color. Where the warm colors of softly illuminated areas merge with cold dark colors, blending needs to be delicately handled to avoid unpleasant muddy colors or a garish effect.

I enjoy painting night scenes. There appears to be something magical about their departure from the conventional that invariably makes a favorable impression on the client. Maybe it's a latent werewolf tendency.

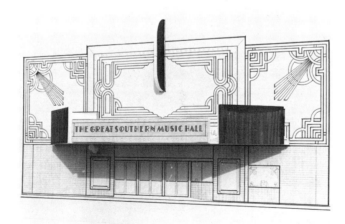

Rosie O'Grady's of Orlando, Florida

City of Orlando Municipal Auditorium. Architects: Tom Price/Don Duer, Winter Park, Florida

Great Southern Music Hall. Architect: Rafael Moreu, Orlando, Florida

Flagship Bank, Orlando, Florida. Architect: Gene Leedy, Winter Haven, Florida

When rendering structures of this kind, it's an advantage to have some appreciation of the architect's philosophies. Mr. Leedy's innovative work enjoys a rightful international reputation. His system of screen walls and concrete T-beams with rough finished structure exposed, express a powerful, solid architectural statement. Some degree of feeling for this should be maintained throughout the rendering process if any justice is to be done to the concepts.

One feature of the design here, is the use of planting. Gene specifies special plants that grow down from the planting boxes and vines that grow up the concrete block columns to compliment some of the building's toughness. This thought was carried through when painting the sky by using whispy cirrus clouds as a foil to the building's solidity. The sky was painted in the manner described on page 80.

The rendering here is a good example of a procedure common to many renderings that I'd like to deal with. We've painted the background, then in front of this we've added the middle distance—the building itself. The next

Same size detail

step is to complete the picture by adding the foreground elements — road, cars, people etc. Before embarking on this however, take what the outstanding instructor/writer Joe Singer calls the "vital pause."

The colors in our picture so far have been dictated by the materials specified. Here, they're the cold colors of solar gray glass and concrete; in other buildings the warm colors of bronze glass and wood may predominate. In either case, if it's felt at this stage that the effect is too monochromatic, complimentary colors need to be used in the final stages to bring the picture back in to balance.

I painted the road here on the warm side of neutral using a mixture of light red, cerulean blue, yellow ochre and phthalo green. The figures and cars were then added in a range of warm tones.

The 'black-top' of roads and parking lots can account for a large area in renderings of public buildings. Not the most pleasant material, but it's there and has to be depicted. Don't make it appear too neutral and drearily flat. Paint in uneven patches that follow its plane, add tire marks, give it some character.

pencil

This has long been the architect's medium. Pencil delineation evolved to heights of preeminence during the early part of the century through the sheer mastery of architect/artists like Thornton Bishop, Chester Price and Otto Eggars. The tradition was to be upheld later by the genius of Schell Lewis and Ted Kautzky.

A romantic involvement with pencil endures to this day within the profession, thanks in no small measure to the legacy of Ted Kautzky's books. His broadpoint technique, enunciated so well in these highly acclaimed books, has become the reference point for delineators ever since.

You have before you, a broadpoint pencil rendering drawn by one of the finest exponents of the medium — the late Robert S. Davis. Bob was Professor of Architecture at the University of Florida for 12 years up to his untimely death in 1971.

Observe the painterly manner in which the pencil is applied and the way he expressed the texture, rich values and outlines of foliage with crisp individual strokes.

Just look at the canopy effect of those trees. Note the feeling of the distances to the ones further away. Consummate control of tonal expression is required to achieve those qualities.

Accounts of Bob's greatness, both as an artist and teacher, are legend. An architect who had the good fortune to work with him once told me that he was ambidextrous and that while drawing foliage with one hand he'd be sketching in things like figures with the other.

Now that makes you sick!

Architect:
Ernest Wolfman AIA., Orlando, Florida

131

These are from a series drawn at the conceptual stage of the U.S. Naval Base, Kings Bay, Georgia. Several architectural themes and palettes were being proposed—a feeling-out process that involved some eighty renderings, with several developed later in tempera.

Pencil on tracing vellum is an ideal medium for this type of presentation where it's desirable to establish a conformity running through the series. To this end, the drawings were handled in the same vignette treatment and from a pedestrian viewpoint.

With a coordinated series like this, a slide show made up of shots in varying degrees of close-up and projected in proper sequence, makes an extremely effective presentation.

Architects: Gunn & Meyerhoff/Rogers & Lopatka,
Savannah Georgia, and Winter Park Florida

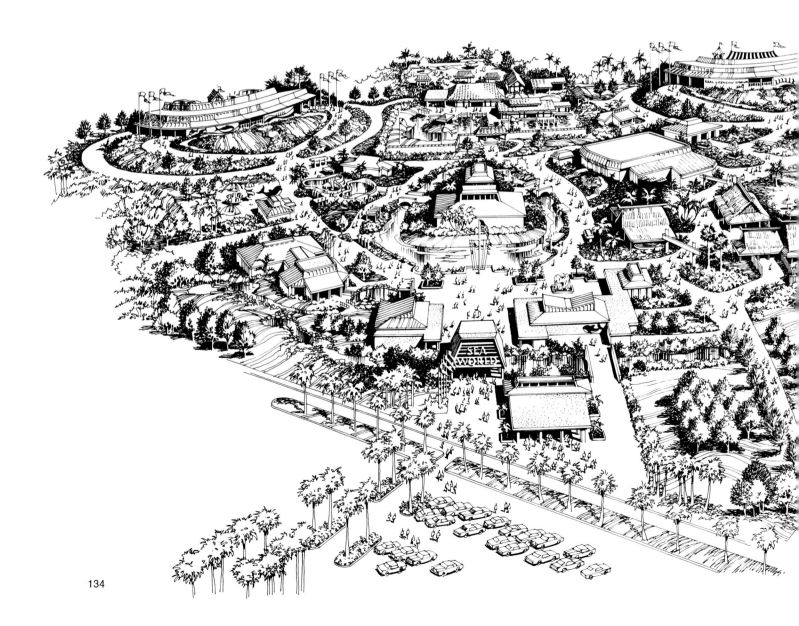

Client: Sea World of Florida, Orlando, Florida

This rendering of Sea World, Orlando, Fla., was started some years ago, then added to at each stage of the attraction's expansion. It's fulfilled a variety of functions over the years.

The original drawing was done after completion of the first phase of construction. This was used in promotional brochures, full page advertisements and as an 'in park' guide for visitors.

In the latter function, areas of tone were dictated by the requirement that visitors be able to relate to the various buildings in finding their way around the park.

When features such as restaurants and the stadium/theater were proposed later, they were drawn in correct location on prints of the original. This was then used to supplement eye-level casein renderings at the presentations.

The original layout was constructed from a series of photographs taken from a helicopter. A hundred or so ground level pictures were also referred to for more detailed information.

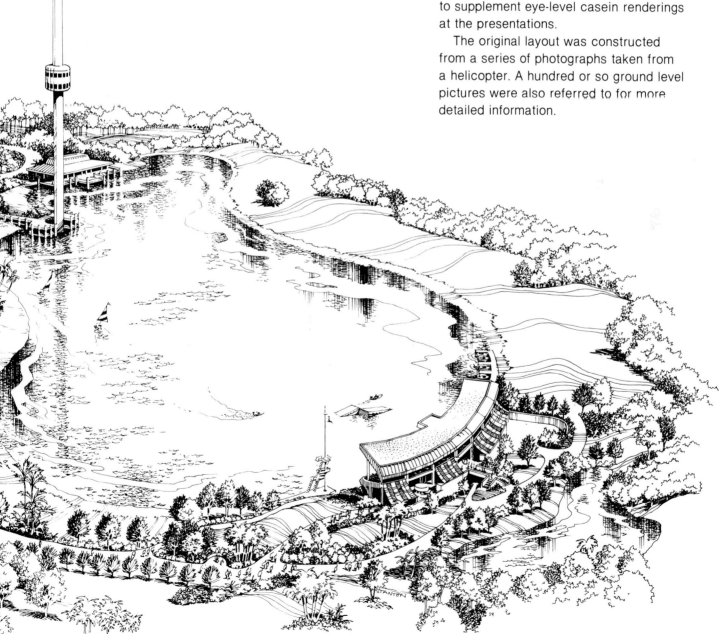

Collection, Mr. and Mrs. Robert C. Feil

Collection, Mr. and Mrs. J. Cubberley

existing buildings

The special knowledge of architectural principles required to render buildings yet to be built, gives the delineator a distinct edge when depicting existing buildings. I like to start with a pencilled perspective just as much detailed as for a regular rendering. The methods of subdividing areas described on pages 34-37 are very useful when reconstructing perspectives from photographs or sketches. Even though architectural accuracy may not be the prime motivation of the picture, I like to do it justice if only out of respect for the art. After painting regular renderings having the same old perfect weather, I enjoy trying to capture a certain mood and establish definite conditions—of weather, time of day and season.

The painting of the White House was done from slides. I'd taken them while keeping vigil along with a few hundred others during events unprecedented in the nation's history. For several days the capital had been blanketed by grey skies and drizzle that matched the mood.

I was walking across the Ellipse the next morning, the first day of a new administration. No sooner had the White House come into view when, as if on cue, the cloud cover began breaking up before a fresh breeze. The house sparkled in the sudden release of sunlight—as if to symbolize the optimism of a fresh clean start. That was the way I had to paint it.

The evergreen was pulled in at the right to provide a foreground framing element. Otherwise the specific tree locations precluded too much license being taken. I was stuck with Andrew Jackson's magnolias blocking off a good portion of the house for instance. These were capitalized on however by painting them very dark to accentuate the building's whiteness.

The line drawing at left is of the Owens-Thomas House, Savannah, Georgia, one of the finest examples of the Regency Period in the United States. Spring showers had darkened the color of the stucco on the building and the bark of the live oaks. What attracted me was the way this heightened their contrast with the bright green of the new growth, giving them almost a blossom quality. The drawing was made from several photos and sketches, using felt-tip pens.

I also tried to create the feeling of an early Spring morning in the watercolor of the Parson Capen House, Topsfield, Mass. To give the effect of a shower having just passed, I gave the roof a wet look and illuminated the scene with characteristic watery sunlight. The retreating shower itself was suggested by painting the sky with directional wet-on-wet strokes. The distant trees were added while the background was still wet to give the effect of seeing them through the rain.

Collection, Mr. and Mrs. A. Langford

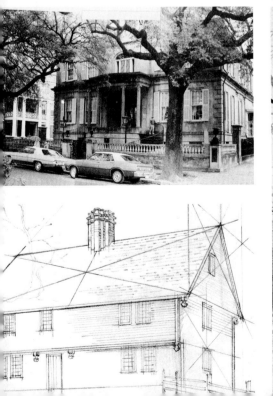

Finally, here are two approaches not covered by any of the categories so far.

Below, a rendering technique was used to render a site plan transferred directly from the architect's drawings. With no perspective being involved, the illusion of depth was achieved mainly with strong shadows. Supplementing a rendered site plan with regular renderings taken from other angles results in a very effective sales tool. The combination has the assets of a model with none of the drawbacks.

The series of renderings opposite, proved to be a storybook case.

My client had been trying for some considerable time to dispose of a sizeable parcel of land adjacent to a theme park. Verbal descriptions and photographs just hadn't been adequate. After kicking the problem around during the wee small hours, (over wee small drinks, in my wee small pool, at an enormous price) Bob Kingsland and I came up with this solution.

The presentation consisted of a casein rendering of the site and surroundings as they stood. Conceptual phases of development were then painted on acetate overlays and superimposed in sequence over the original.

Armed with this presentation, Bob got on a plane to California and proceeded to sell the property at the first showing.

And that, my dear friends, is what this fabulous business is all about.

Fountainbrook Townhomes. Architect: Architects Design Group, Winter Park, Florida

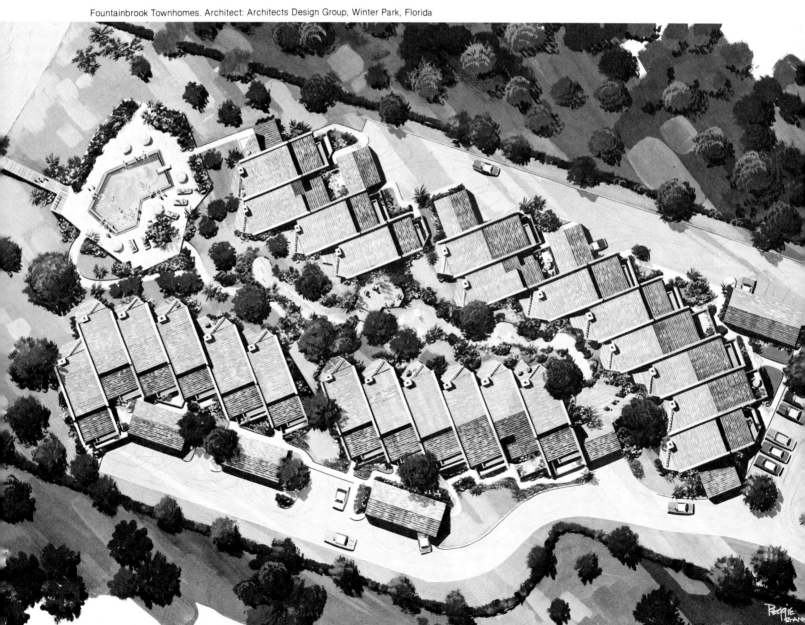

Kingsland-Henry & Assoc., Winter Park, Florida

the business

Having hopefully passed on to you a measure of guidance enabling you to produce a marketable product, I'm not about to take my leave without offering some thoughts on peddling said merchandise, based on what I've learned.

With all there is to learn about rendering (cripes, you could write a book on the subject), the thing that seems to concern the beginner far more than anything else is what to charge. My advice is don't waste time being too preoccupied with this aspect. Just be totally honest with yourself in assessing your abilities and where you stand in the marketplace. You have to strike the right balance. If you try to command high prices too soon, you may only succeed in slamming shut some doors that will be difficult to get a foot into later. Work too cheaply and you'll set a precedent that will be difficult to break out of.

Be content in the knowledge that those handsome fees you've heard about will come naturally—when the quality of your work justifies them. So what if they arrive a little later than expected? Look—you're getting paid for something you enjoy doing. You know an awful lot of people live out their entire lives without ever being able to say that.

So relax. Let the prospect of quality fees be an incentive to develop a quality product, acquire a reputation for dependability along the way—and you'll be fighting clients off in no time.

Operating from a posture of confidence in quality, price and service will prove to be an asset when dealing with the many people who feel obligated to haggle over terms with *everyone* — let alone a freelance artist!

Adopt a system of fair and reasonable pricing and stick to it. Don't just pull price quotations out of the air or charge what you think the client can afford. I've found the fairest method is to base prices on a certain hourly rate. This automatically correlates your prices to some extent with those of construction. See that the client appreciates for instance, the difference between painting a complicated all-brick building and a simple stucco one, and realizes that renderings aren't sold by the square inch.

Three factors are pertinent to the transaction — quality, price and delivery time. Quality is already established or you wouldn't be discussing the other two. Reserve the right to name at least one of the others, it's dumb business to allow the client to name both price and delivery. Try it with a car salesman some time.

An architect may tell you that he's already quoted his client a certain figure that is below what yours would have been. You feel obligated to honor the quote and let it slide — it could be an honest mistake, perhaps he hasn't bought a rendering for a couple of years. But if the same guy pulls this one again, you'd better tell him that if he promises to quit this practice, you'll promise not to tell his clients what they should pay him.

It's a good policy to discuss fees only with the person who's doing the buying — the owner, senior executives or official buyer. Your fee may be equivalent to a junior associate's monthly salary, eliciting a reaction that gets in the way of a good working relationship (the fact that you'll have to exist on three hours sleep for a few nights to meet the deadline, will be completely overlooked). Spare him the pain. Phone in your quote to his boss later.

Sometimes, for a valued client, I'll throw in a quick rendering for free if there's a possibility it will help him land a job. But beware of this guy: — "All I need is a little sketch . . ." — "Just dash off something real quick . . ." — "My budget won't run to the proper thing right now, but later . . . . . ."

Boy, the times a freelancer hears it. By all means give the chap a break if you think he's genuinely down on his luck. But what started out as a quick rough squeezed into an already overloaded schedule, can turn into: — "Take that tree out . . ." — "Put more cars in . . ." — "Make one my gold Mercedes with a sunroof . . ."

Before you know it, he's got a Rolls-Royce rendering at a Tinker Toy trade-in-price — Johnny Carson is into his monologue and the job must be in the client's boardroom at 8 a.m. sharp still requires hours of work.

Oh — if you're lucky, you may get paid for that 'quickie' but the check will probably be a 'slowie'. Isn't it great owning your own business? And this was on Labor Day. There are some days when artists simply have more fun than people.

Be business-like. Submit invoices promptly and follow them up. When you've given good dependable service you have every right to expect reciprocal consideration. A good buyer will take care of his suppliers in this regard. Never invoice for more than the quotation, except where unanticipated extra work is involved — rather it be the other way round. Keep accurate records of every job on file.

One of the many bonuses of this business is that architects are great folks to work with. Their profession requires them to be good communicators and precise in their specifications. You'll work better with them and gain their confidence by learning and using correct architectural terminology.

Try to assemble all information on a job at one meeting. Nothing shakes a client's confidence in you more than constantly being called to the phone.

You'll be working with many other great business people. Learn from them at every opportunity.

It's important to conduct your business on a professional level and maintain high ethical standards. Cultivate a reputation for absolute discretion. You'll be working with many firms all competing with each other. Whether it's a multi-million dollar job or a couple of thousand, what one client is doing is no one else's business. Suggestions that a confidence be breached should be rejected out of hand with a reminder that, by the same token, theirs will be respected too.

Some projects can involve millions of dollars with all manner of ramifications for various interest groups. Protecting confidentiality may require working behind locked doors for a time, even away from your own family.

Your prosperity is linked to that of your clients. Delivery of renderings need not be the end of your involvement. Show an interest in the subsequent stages of the project's development. Take time out to drive over and visit the finished building. You'll get a feel for the way the company operates and be in a position to contribute thoughts of mutual benefit at future sales-approach conferences.

I've thoroughly enjoyed our visit together.

This unique field of graphic communication has been extremely rewarding to me in every sense. It is my sincere wish that this guide will help the reader attain experiences as richly fulfilling.

credits

These illustrations are reproduced by permission of: —
Alinari/SCALA, 10
Watson-Guptill Publications, 13
McGraw-Hill Book Company, 14
Van Nostrand Reinhold Company, 18
Graphic Indicator Company, 18
Graphicraft, 19
PPG Industries, Inc., 48 (1)
California Redwood Association, 50

All photographs by the author except: —
Esquire Photographers, 86, 92, 93, 94, 96, 98, 140
Theodore Flagg, 8, 40, 58
D.G. Williams, 42-43